# SWING TRADING

## OLIVER L. VELEZ

Marketplace Books
Columbia, Maryland

This book, along with other books, is available at discounts that make it realistic to provide them as gifts to your customers, clients, and staff. For more information on these long lasting, cost effective premiums, please call us at 800-272-2855 or e-mail us at sales@traderslibrary.com.

ISBN: 1-59280-315-6
ISBN 13: 978-1-59280-315-6
Printed in the United States of America.

Table of Contents

# Swing Trading

# FROM THE PUBLISHER

The editors at Marketplace Books have always kept a steady goal in mind, and that is to present actionable information on stock trading in the most straight-forward, practical medium available. Sometimes this involves a book, sometimes a newsletter, a DVD, or an online course program. What we've learned from the many products we've developed over the years is that a cross-medium approach is the most effective way to offer the greatest possible value to our readers.

So an idea was born. This innovative book and DVD set is one of the first in a series that combines a full course book derived from the actual presentation itself. Our idea grew out of a simple question. Students of stock trading spend a great deal of their own money attending lectures and trade shows. After all the travel, effort, and expense, that student will still have to assimilate a host of often complex theories and strategies. Sometimes he or she may want to ask a question or dig deeper into an issue, but they hold back; maybe because they still don't know enough about the bigger picture or maybe they don't even know some of the basic terminology. They may buy the DVD, but still…a lecture in itself is not a comprehensive learning tool and a person may still need yet another lecture or host of trial and error book purchases to master the subject.

So the question was: Does the average student of trading get enough out of an individual session to effectively carry their studies home and master a subject? The answer was a resounding no! Most attendees get bits and pieces of the message out of a long and expensive lineage of lectures, with critical details hopefully captured in page after page of scribbled notes. For those who are gifted with a photographic memory and vast organizational skills, the visual lecture is just fine, but for the rest of us, the combination of the written word and a visual demonstration is the golden ticket to the mastery of any subject.

A comprehensive approach to learning is the course you are about to embark upon. We've taken Oliver Velez's original lecture and extracted his core content into an easy to read and understand course book. You'll be able to pour over every word of Velez's groundbreaking presentation, taking in each important point in a step by step, layer by layer process. All of this is possible because our editors have developed this title in classic textbook form. We've organized and highlighted the key points, added case studies, glossaries, key terms, and even an index so you can go to the information you need when you need it most.

Let's face it, stock trading in any medium takes years to master. It takes time to be able to follow charts and pick out the indicators that mark the wins you'll need to succeed. And beyond the mathematical details and back-tested chart patterns, every presenter has three very basic premises for every student trader; they are to control your emotions, stay close to your trading plan, and do your homework. It's so important to know the full picture of the profession because it could either make you rich or put you in line for that second night job.

This DVD course book package is meant to give you all the visual and written reinforcement you need to study, memorize, document, and master your subject once and for all. We think this is a truly unique approach to realizing the full potential of our Traders' Library DVDs.

As always, we wish you the greatest success.

# Meet Oliver Velez

Oliver L. Velez, best selling author, trader, advisor, and entrepreneur, is one of the most sought after speakers and teachers on the subject of trading financial markets for a living. His seminars and speaking events have been attended by more than 60,000 traders all over the world, and his runaway best selling books, *Strategies for Profiting on Every Trade* and *Tools and Tactics of the Master Day Trader*, are considered must-read classics for anyone interested in trading markets for a living. Dow Jones dubbed him "the messiah of day trading" and financial programs on *CNBC*, *Bloomberg* and *Fox News* frequently seek out his expertise. Mr. Velez and his life-long dedication to bringing more awareness to trading as a way of life, have been favorably mentioned in the *New York Times*, the *Wall Street Journal*, *Barron's*, *Forbes*, *Stocks & Commodities* and a whole host of other financial publications. He has also been the subject of numerous articles and books written about Wall Street's most successful traders, including the popular book, *Bulls, Bears and Brains*.

Oliver L. Velez is internationally known for founding and growing Pristine Capital Holdings, Inc. (a firm he started out of his New York City basement apartment) into one of the country's premier educational institutions for investors and self-directed, retail traders. After serving as Pristine's Chairman and CEO for 12 years, Mr. Velez decided to turn his full attention to the professional trading arena. His new training program called Trade for Life™, which includes a 2-day seminar and 5-day Live Trading Session with Mr. Velez himself, is designed to train traders to go beyond retail to trade the markets professionally.

Today, Mr. Velez runs Velez Capital Management, LLC ("VCM"), one of the country's fastest growing private equity trading firms. VCM currently employs 260 professional traders who have been meticulously trained to trade his own personal account. Mr. Velez financially backs each one of his traders, absorbing all their losses, while sharing in the gains with the trader. Mr. Velez' vision is to grow his professional team of traders to more than 1,000 globally over the next 3 years. For the past 19 years, he has espoused the revolutionary idea that "micro trading," like "micro banking" has the potential to serve as a solution to many of the world's social ills. Through VCM and the Velez Family Foundation, Mr. Velez will be opening up trading divisions and training centers in Beijing, Vietnam, Moscow and Mexico City. More major cities throughout the world will be added in the future.

# SWING TRADING

# Chapter 1

# What is Swing Trading?

## The Reality of Stock Trading

Let's start with a discussion on the concept of trading. Trading is nothing more than the art of finding two groups of ill-informed market players; those willing to give up their merchandise to you too inexpensively, and those willing to take it off of your hands at a price you know is too expensive. So in reality, we are taking advantage of ignorance. To be more specific, we are taking advantage of two emotions at work—fear (which is often driven by pain) and greed. These two emotions are what make stock prices move. If you can find someone who is in enough pain you will usually find someone who is willing to give up their merchandise too inexpensively. Find someone with enough greed and you will usually find someone who is willing to pay too much for your merchandise.

> The emotions of fear and greed are what drive the price of anything that can be bought and sold in an open market.

## Trading Versus Investing

You notice that I am using the word trading and have not used the term investing. That does not mean to imply that positions cannot be held for long periods of time, even months and years in some cases. We use the term trading because it implies the use of management techniques to monitor positions whether they are long term or short term positions. The term investing implies the old-fashioned "buy and hold" strategy that I consider to be a dead concept. The reason for this is simple. Things have changed in the marketplace.

Years ago the main capitalization of the stock market was in manufacturing. Automobiles, steel and heavy-duty, machinery were the stocks that drove the market. If someone wanted to start up a new car company and drive General Motors out of business, it would have been an incredible undertaking. It would have required vast amounts of money and more importantly, large amounts of time. Today things are different, very different. The main capitalization of the stock market today is in technology and services. The difference today is that "two kids in a garage" can bring any big company to its knees overnight.

A great example of this concept can be found in the story of a little company called Iomega. Not long ago computers were growing at

> While longer-term positions can be perfectly fine if managed properly, the term "investing" as is commonly used is a dead term, in my opinion.

an exponential pace and the need for methods of backing up more and more data became critical. This was back in the days where the 1.4 MB diskettes were the only answer. Then along came Iomega. They created a storage device that held approximately seventy times the data and fit into the same space in the same area of the computer. The stock went from being a penny-stock to a single-digit stock to topping out well over $60. During this time they received a contract to go on every manufacturer's computer as standard equipment. They had a unique product and a virtual monopoly so it is no wonder why their stock price accelerated so quickly. This stock certainly seemed like a stock you would bring home for the grand kids. That is until one weekend when "two kids in a garage" discovered that four to five times the information could be stored on a CD-ROM for a fraction of the price. What happens to Iomega that Monday morning? Unless they have another product to offer, they are virtually out of business, and that is precisely what happened. Those managing their position as a trader would have preserved most of their profits. A buy and hold investor would have given up all their profits. The Iomega story can apply to hundreds of stocks in recent times. If you held stocks long during the 2000 - 2002 crash, I don't have to explain much further. The world moves quickly and does not wait for investors who get married to their stocks.

## Swing Trading Involves Timing

When we talk about swing trading, we're talking about a subset of the broader category of trading. It is a unique style of market play that involves an overlooked niche. It involves holding a stock anywhere from two to five trading days. Oftentimes a swing trade can last as long as ten days, but on average it's about a two to five day trade. What's interesting about this style and philosophy of trading is that it helps to capitalize on a market niche that in my opinion is still largely overlooked by some of your bigger players in the market.

Consider this concept. The two to five day timeframe is too lengthy for day traders who typically never hold a stock overnight, and at the same time it's too short for those very large institutions to take advantage of. So that means two of the most dominant market groups in existence today are really not involved in this two to five day timeframe.

The big elephants, the institutions, cannot maneuver quickly enough for a two to five day timeframe. Their large purchases and sales must be done over a longer time. Day traders, market makers, and specialists do not typically hold stocks overnight. The individual astute swing trader operating in this void is devoid of serious competition. Basically he or she is operating in a timeframe

> The two to five day holding time of the swing trade finds a unique niche in the market.

or a pocket in the market that really only has as participants ill-informed market players.  And that spells opportunity.

## Trading Emotions

I am a firm believer of the fact that we do not trade stocks.  We trade people. And what moves people? Emotions do; and what we are trading against are the two most dominant emotions—fear and greed.

To really drive this point home, understand that there are only three major emotions at work in the market, period. The three emotions are fear, greed, and uncertainty.

If you become a master at pinpointing when one emotion turns into another emotion, you've got the game conquered.

When the dominant market players are uncertain, stocks tend to consolidate. Go nowhere. Basically they vacillate between a relatively predictable price range. When fear is the dominant emotion shared by the dominant group in the stock, the

*We don't trade stocks, we trade people.*

stock will trend lower. When the majority of the individual players in an individual stock are experiencing greed, this stock will trend higher.

## The Importance of Understanding the Market

Here is another point I'd like to make clear before we proceed. The equity market, or the stock market, is a wealth-creating mechanism unlike the futures market. The futures market is really and truly a zero sum game; some would actually call it a minus sum game when you add commissions to the factor. What that really means is that the futures market is a wealth-robbing mechanism while the equity market is a wealth-creating mechanism. This is incredibly important to understand before we actually delve into the concepts of swing trading. I'll explain why.

In the futures market, everyone puts in or contributes to the kitty. If we were all futures traders in the same vehicle, we'd have to pull our money out, each one of us, and add our money to the kitty. What this means is that whenever an individual wins, he has subtracted wealth from the kitty. In other words, in order to have a winner, we must have a loser.

Now, a lot of people erroneously assume that this applies to the equity market. It does not. Not always. The futures market takes wealth away from someone else on every trade. The equity market can create wealth out of thin air.

Let me go over a scenario for you. I buy a stock at ten; sell it to you at twelve. You buy it at twelve and sell it to another at fourteen. They buy it at fourteen and sell it to another at sixteen. Who has lost in that scenario? No one. Let's say that person takes it at sixteen and sells it to another at eighteen, who sells it to another at twenty. They take it at twenty and sell it to someone else at twenty-two. No losers. This continues until somebody buys the stock at, let's say, thirty dollars. Now this person who bought at thirty goes looking for someone to pay thirty-two. But all of a sudden, for some reason there are no takers at thirty two. This gentleman is looking for his greater fool. But there is no greater fool. He decides he better try finding somebody at thirty one, but once again there are no takers.

At that point he realizes that he has potentially made a mistake, and now what was greed that incited him to buy at thirty, now starts to convert itself to the emotion of uncertainty. From uncertainty, fear starts to creep in and sit right on his shoulder. And fear asks, "Do you remember what happened the last time you hung around?"

So what happens is this individual says, "Yes, I do remember and it wasn't a pleasant experience." So he starts looking for someone to take it from him at twenty-eight. He sells it to someone at twenty-eight. Someone at twenty-eight looks for someone at twenty-nine. No longer being able to find someone at twenty-nine, he feels he's made a mistake. His greed has turned into uncertainty then to fear as well and now he's selling at twenty-six. Someone takes it at twenty-six, sells it at twenty-four because he can't find someone at twenty-five and the process reverses itself.

Our job is to be able to pinpoint when that last person at twenty-five has trapped himself. That is the guy that I want. Because what I want to do is squeeze his stock away from him. I want to see such a panic that it will cause him to search out an exit from the stock he just entered, at twenty-four or twenty-three. I want to incite this individual to sell his stock to me at the very moment he should actually be thinking about buying more.

This is true professional trading. Swing trading offers the ability to take advantage of that switch from greed to uncertainty, to fear to uncertainty, to greed to uncertainty, to fear to uncertainty, to greed over and over again in an easier fashion than your typical day trading does.

## Why is Swing Trading Better?

I believe swing trading is much safer than traditional day trading simply because the individual has more time to filter information. The individual has more time to make informed decisions. The individual has more time to assess the environment. Under those circumstances more intelligent decisions can be made. I find that the typical day trader, especially the micro trader without a great deal of seasoning, cannot act intelligently when he has a fraction of a second to do so. Swing trading is also safer than day trading simply because it lends itself to diversification, which is not usually the case when micro trading. Micro traders are going after exceptionally small gains so they have to make up for those small gains and the commissions that are levied against them with larger share size. That means, in many cases, piling into one play for a few seconds to a few minutes with the hope of capturing a small, micro gain. That takes a level of precision that most traders do not ever obtain because that type of precision and accuracy is only obtained through a long period of experience in the market. Finally, it is my contention that swing trading is even safer than investing. There is far less time for those all-too-often negative surprises to occur.

So swing trading is safer because it lends itself to diversification and because it lends itself to playing that style with a smaller account. Even as a talented market player, in order for me to put the odds in my favor when day trading, I have to play a big size; therefore, I have to have a big account. When swing trading, I can play fractional amounts because I'm capturing larger gains.

# Self-test questions

1. In swing trading theory, what moves the market?

   a. Fear and greed
   b. Intelligent traders
   c. Well-run companies with innovative products
   d. The "tape"

2. What is the significance of market capitalization shifting from the manufacturing sector to technology and services sectors?

   a. Manufacturing companies are no longer good trading vehicles
   b. The economy is about to expand exponentially
   c. "Two kids in a garage" can now take on the auto mobile industry
   d. Buy-and-hold investing is dead and stocks now must be actively managed and traded

3. Which statement is false about swing trading techniques?

   a. Larger institutional traders can't trade on the swing trading time frame
   b. It's less risky than daytrading
   c. It has smaller risks but requires a larger account
   d. It's an unexploited niche

4. According to Oliver Velez, what is trading really about?

    a. Money management
    b. Careful analysis of all economic conditions
    c. Trading people
    d. Taking advantage of market inefficiencies in bid/ask prizes

5. In stock trading fear causes:

    a. Stock prices to go up
    b. Stock prices to go down
    c. Money to flow out of the market
    d. Daytraders to become greedy

6. Why can I exploit fear and greed?

    a. Because I can pinpoint these areas on a stock chart and use them to my advantage
    b. Because only inexperienced traders feel these emotions
    c. Not necessary, unlike futures, stock trading is not a "zero sum" game—we can all win
    d. Because the helpless are always there to be exploited

For answers, go to www.traderslibrary.com/TLEcorner

# Chapter 2

# The Time Horizons

## The Pristine System and Timing Methods

Before we get into swing trading, it is important that you understand the timeframes that are available and where swing trading fits in. This way you can stick to the timeframe you select. The Pristine Method® of Trading makes six major timeframes available to its practitioners. These can be grouped into three broad categories. They are long term, intermediate term, and short term.

## The Long Term Timeframe

The long term timeframe consists of yearly and monthly charts. A yearly chart is a chart where every bar represents one year of trading. The yearly chart is used primarily for cyclical analysis and

FIGURE 2.1- **Monthly Chart**

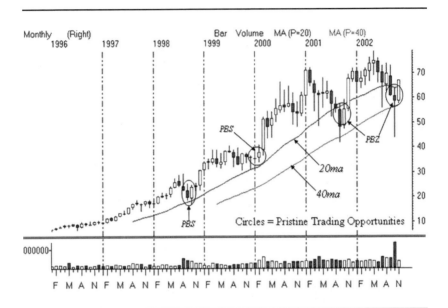

sometimes for long-term trading. On the monthly chart every bar represents one month of trading, or approximately twenty trading days. As a swing trader you will review the monthly charts of all stocks in your universe at least once a month. The monthly chart is an excellent chart for longer-term trading, and the swing trader may use monthly charts to help find longer-term trends. Figure 2.1 is an example of a monthly chart.

The vertical dotted lines represent the years and the scale along the bottom lets you know that every bar represents one month.

FIGURE 2.2 - **Weekly Chart**

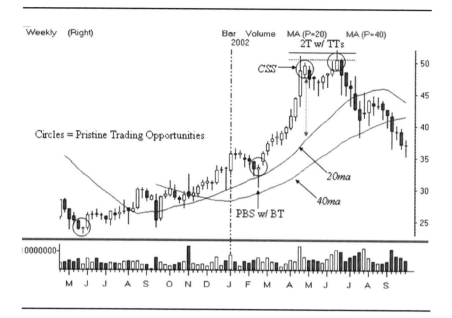

## The Intermediate Timeframe

The next timeframe is the intermediate term timeframe, which consists of weekly and daily charts. The weekly chart is the key chart used by longer-term traders and will be the source of 85% of their plays. On the weekly chart every bar represents one week or five days worth of trading. Figure 2.2 is an example of a weekly chart.

## The Daily Timeframe

The daily chart is the home for the swing trader. Eighty-five percent of the swing trader's trades will originate from the daily chart. Every night the swing trader will review his or her universe of stocks through the eyes the daily chart. Let's take a look at the daily chart in Figure 2.3.

The daily chart is the most common chart you will see if you are not an active trader. Every bar represents one day's worth of trading. Notice that the bars and the overall flow of the chart are the

**FIGURE 2.3 - Daily Chart**

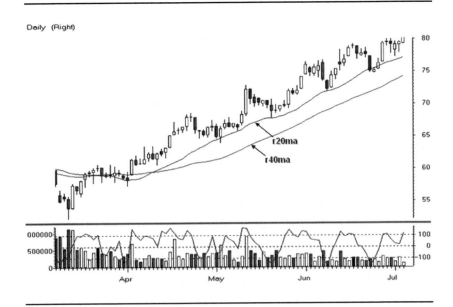

For color charts go to www.traderslibrary.com/TLEcorner

A trader's universe of stocks is a subset of all tradable stocks that includes the biggest total list of stocks that a trader would ever use for trading.

same as a weekly chart or a monthly chart. This is true of all charts, even intraday charts. The Pristine Method® works equally as well on any timeframe because we're trading people, not stocks, as we discussed earlier. These charts all use Japanese candlesticks as the charting technique. I do not consider a chart a chart unless it is displayed in Japanese candlesticks. We'll be discussing the use of these candlesticks shortly.

Notice also the two moving averages on this chart. They are the simple 20-period moving average and the simple 40-period moving average. These two moving averages are staples that should be on all of your longer-term charts. They are used as trend-setting tools the help us determine the nature and quality of the trend of any particular stock. You will see shortly that between the Japanese candlesticks and these two moving averages, we will have virtually all of the tools we need for swing trading effectively.

The 20- and 40-period simple moving averages should be staples on all your charts.

Next we have the short term timeframe. This timeframe consists of hourly charts and other intraday charts such as the 15-minute and 5-minute charts. Take a look at the hourly chart in Figure 2.4.

FIGURE 2.4 -Hourly Chart

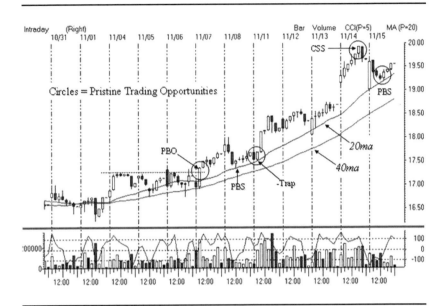

For color charts go to www.traderslibrary.com/TLEcorner

Here every bar represents one hour's worth of trading. The vertical lines here represent the breaks from one day to the next. Note that different trading platforms show slight differences because of the fact that there are six and a half hours in every trading day. You may opt to start your hourly charts at 9:00 Eastern Standard Time or 9:30 Eastern Standard Time and, depending upon your choice,

> The hourly chart is a very versatile chart that can be used by swing and intraday traders.

FIGURE 2.5 - 5 Minute Chart

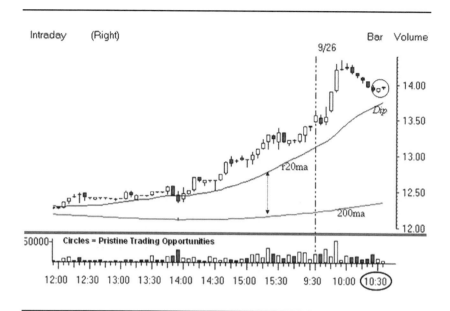

there will be a slight difference in the final result. There is no uniform agreement on which is appropriate.

The hourly chart is an incredible chart. It is versatile in that it can be used for short term hits by swing traders, and it serves as an excellent alternative in choppy environments for one to two day holds. It is also used widely by the intraday trader to help determine the trend of the current day.

Here are examples of intraday charts, namely the 5-minute and 15-minute chart as shown in Figures 2.5 and 2.6. Again the verti-

FIGURE 2.6 -15 Minute Chart

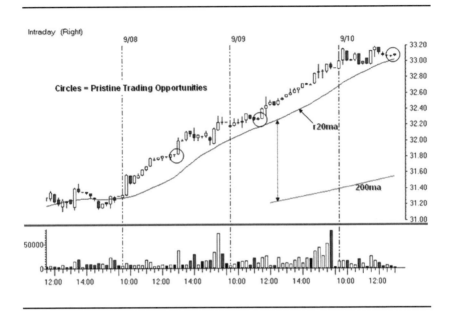

cal lines represent the day breaks. These charts are used primarily by day traders and occasionally to refine management in longer-term trades.

## The Wealth and Income Building Styles

The use of these charts makes available four major styles of trading. These four major styles of trading can be grouped into two broad categories. They are known as the wealth building style and income producing style.

*The Wealth Building Style:* The wealth building style includes core trading and swing trading. Core traders primarily use the weekly charts for holding periods ranging from a few weeks to many months. This is the long-term style of trading and differs from investing because all trades will always be managed and never left to the "buy and hold" mentality. Swing traders will primarily use the daily chart and look for holding times from two to five days, and occasionally out to ten days.

*The Income Producing Style:* The income producing style of trading includes guerrilla trades and intraday trades. Guerilla trades refer to a specific set of hit-and-run type tactics that range from swing trading off of the hourly chart to a list of very specific trading tactics that Pristine traders use. Intraday trading is also referred to as day trading and also includes the subset of micro trading. All have in common the fact that traders will be exiting all positions by the end of the day.

If you're going to be trading the markets full time it is important to understand that you need to be involved in both the wealth building and income producing styles of trading. The reason for this is because when markets are trending up or down and experiencing very strong moves, the vast majority of money is made from longer-term positions and longer-term holds. When markets tend to go sideways for long periods of time, it can become difficult to produce wealth from longer-term trading. Traders who are able to produce income on shorter time periods to supplement the longer-term moves of the market will have an advantage over those who are restricted to one type of trading.

# Self-test questions

1. In how many timeframes can the Pristine Method be used?

   a. Yearly
   b Monthly
   c. Daily
   d. Intraday
   e. All of the above

2. Which is the most useful for a swing trader?

   a. Intraday
   b. Daily
   c. Weekly
   d. Monthly
   e. All of the above

3. If you are wealth-building, which timeframe would you be most interested in?

   a. Yearly
   b. Monthly
   c. Daily
   d. Intraday
   e. All of the above

4. How can you tell a yearly chart from an intraday chart?

    a. Intraday charts have wider-ranging bars
    b. There are more bars on an intraday chart
    c. They all look alike; you have to check the chart's scale
    d. The longer-time frame has a smoother chart pattern

5. How does Velez use moving averages in swing trading?

    a. Buy/sell signals
    b. Establishing a trend
    c. Finding the "true" stock price
    d. Setting stops

**For answers, go to www.traderslibrary.com/TLEcorner**

# Chapter 3

# The Japanese Candlestick Chart

Let's take a look of some of the tools needed by the swing trader. First of all, notice on all of the charts I have shown you, Japanese candlesticks are used. A price chart is not a price chart to me unless it is displayed in Japanese candlestick form. Technically, a Japanese candlestick does not display any more information than a regular bar chart. They both display the opening, closing, high, and low of that particular period. The difference is that the Japanese candlesticks display the information in a way that is much easier to see visually. The area between the high low is colored either red (black or closed) or green (white or open) depending upon whether the stock closed above or below its opening price. This places the emphasis on who won the battle each and every time period.

> Charts can be displayed in a line form, a bar form, or several other forms. The Japanese candlestick shows the information better visually than other methods.

A good example of this difference was seen on the day Microsoft gapped up five dollars. From the moment the stock opened it began selling off and continued to drop steadily throughout the day until it had lost three and a half dollars of the morning gap. Late in the afternoon the star of one of our favorite cable shows was giving her afternoon run-down and reported in an elated voice that, "traders

---

**FIGURE 3.1 - Understanding Candlesticks**

---

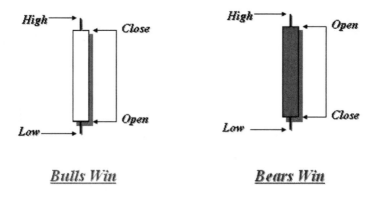

## *Determining Who Won The Battle*

*Bulls Win*          *Bears Win*

---

For color charts go to www.traderslibrary.com/TLEcorner

---

were buying up Microsoft all day long as the stock was trading one and a half dollars higher." While it is true that the stock was still up one and a half dollars, the true sentiment of the stock was very bearish as it had lost almost all of its opening gain.

This also allows for much more efficient scanning when looking for many of the patterns that I look for. Take a look at the examples of these two Japanese candlesticks in Figure 3.1.

Their black and white boxes represent the open and closing prices for that time. When the stock closes above its opening price the bulls have won that session and the box is colored white (or green). This is known as the body of the candlestick. The lines extending from the top and bottom of the body represent the high and low for that time period. These are called wicks, tails, or shadows. The second candle is black (or red) because the bears won the battle for this particular period of time. They were able to close the stock at the price at which it opened.

Figure 3.2 shows examples of five different bullish candles. They are all considered bullish because the body is white as the bulls closed the price above the opening price.

It is important to understand that while all of these candles are white, there is a great degree of difference in the bullishness of the candles. When the opening and closing price are very close together, the significance of black or white becomes less important. In these cases, the size and position of the tail becomes as important as the color of the candle. In the examples above, the first and

FIGURE 3.2 - Understanding Candlesticks- Bulls Win

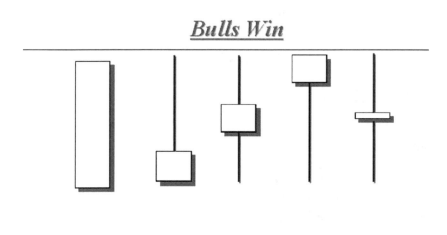

## *Bulls Win*

For color charts go to www.traderslibrary.com/TLEcorner

fourth candles are very bullish not simply because of their white bars but because they closed at the high of the days range. While the second candle is white, it can actually be considered somewhat of a bearish candle. This is because the white body is very small, and there is a huge topping tail sitting on top of the body. This means that at one time, the bulls had run the stock all the way to the high of the day, as shown by the top of that topping tail. However by the end of the day the bears had run the stock down to near the low of the day. There is some truth in the old adage that novices open the market and professionals close the market.

Topping tails and bottoming tails are the graffiti marks of big sellers and buyers and should be respected.

## The Critical Nature of Volume and Price

The next tool that should be on all of your charts is color-coded volume bars. The understanding of volume in conjunction with price is critical to your success as a trader. Traders who understand these two can make a living in the markets without the need of anything else. Now despite what I just said, the concept of volume is often misunderstood and overused. There are literally entire books written on volume, but when it comes down to it, volume really serves two main purposes. Increases in volume can help identify the beginning of new moves, and they can help identify the ending of old moves. We'll discuss more on volume later.

## The CCI Technical Indicator

Let's take a look at another tool of the swing trader. It is a technical indicator known as the CCI, which is an abbreviation for the Commodity Channel Index. The indicator I like to use on daily charts is the 5-period CCI. In practice, I typically overlay the CCI over my volume on the bottom panel of the chart. Figure 3.3 shows what the CCI looks like all by itself, and how we use it.

FIGURE 3.3 - Commodity Channel Index (CCI)

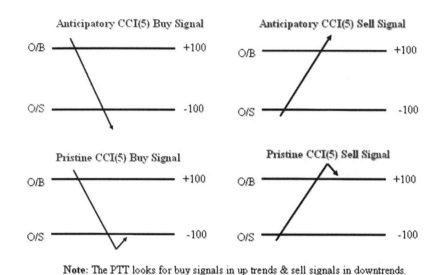

Note: The PTT looks for buy signals in up trends & sell signals in downtrends.

## The Importance of the Buy Setup

We have not discussed the buy setup yet, but I want to introduce you to this tool right now. If we are waiting to buy a stock, we want the CCI to drop below -100. Once it does that, its job is done as it has now "approved" the trade. It does not need to be below -100 at the time you take the trade nor does it need to go above -100 to enter the trade. Notice that while we call this an anticipatory buy setup, it should never be considered a buy on its own. It is only a filter to discard the trade if the CCI does not do what you need it to do.

## The 20- and 40-Period Moving Averages

The other tools we will need are the 20- and 40-period moving averages. These are used to help determine the quality of the trend that the stock is in. We will discuss these as we get to trends in a later section of the book.

## Do Not Get Hooked on a Single Indicator

I am not a big believer in the use, or overuse, of technical indicators. There are charting packages available today that literally contain hundreds of technical indicators. Just the simple fact that there are hundreds available should tell you the value of any one of them. They are often very popular with novice traders because they tend to represent something newcomers to the market like to see. Many new traders are often searching for the Holy Grail of trading. They're looking for that one market guru or that one indicator that will deliver consistent profits time and time again.

Something you need to understand about technical indicators is that they all have one thing in common. They are all taking the past price and volume data on your charts and creating a new line from old data. They have a value in many instances but should never be used to make buy and sell decisions. Traders often find one particular indicator that works on a certain stock for a certain period of time and feel they have found the Holy Grail to trading. However, they soon discover that the indicator needs to be tweaked and adjusted and eventually discarded. For making buy and sell decisions, there is nothing superior to the price pattern itself.

The danger is in feeling that any single indicator will give you consistent profits. I have seen traders use so many indicators, on their charts that it is difficult to even see the price bars through the mess of spaghetti on their chart. Some traders find that one or two particular indicators help them in the process of making a decision and

*Technical indicators should not be the basis for buy and sell decisions.*

that is perfectly fine. Moving averages are actually technical indicators. While they are the simplest of the indicators, they do present us with valuable information. But I do not use moving averages to determine my entry. I use them as a guide to help determine the quality of the trend. The proper use of technical indicators is to use them as a filter. By that I mean once your decision is made to enter a position, you may choose not to because the indicator has not "approved" the trade.

So these tools are all that I have on my charts. They are again, Japanese candlesticks, color-coded volume, the 20- and 40- period moving averages, and the CCI. These are all the tools that are needed to swing trade effectively.

# Self-test questions

1. Prisine traders use Japanese candlesticks because

   a. They are more accurate

   b. They display more information

   c. They are visually easier to read than traditional OHLC bars

   d. Their formations give buy/sell signals

2. The color-coded Japanese candlestick bodies emphasize

   a. Bullish or bearish momentum

   b. Profits and losses

   c. Fear and greed

   d. Entries and exits

3. What are the advantages to using indicators?

   a. They clarify complex chart patterns

   b. They're easy for inexperienced traders to use

   c. They filter out undesirable stocks

   d. They can be adjusted to any type of market

4. Why should I use the CCI (commodity channel index indicator)?

    a. It uses futures prices to determine buy/sell opportunities
    b. It can give technical approval of likely trades
    c. It doesn't need to be tweaked or adjusted
    d. It's been shown to be consistently profitable

5. In Pristine trading which trading tool helps identify the beginning of new moves?

    a. Japanese candlesticks
    b. CCI
    c. Moving averages
    d. Color-coded volume

**For answers, go to www.traderslibrary.com/TLEcorner**

# Chapter 4

# The Market's Basic Unit

## The Foundation of Trading Charts

We are now ready to setup the foundation that will become the basis for trading any chart on any timeframe. There are two parts to this foundation. The first part is what we call the "atom" of a market or a stock's cycle. We also refer to this as the market's or stock's basic unit. The second part of this foundation (market directions) will be discussed in the next chapter.

The following two concepts form the cornerstone of every one of my sound trading techniques and tactics. After gaining a clear understanding of these two building blocks, you should never again find yourself confused and not knowing what to do. In fact, once these two powerful but simple concepts are understood and mas-

FIGURE 4.1 - The Market's Basic Unit/Atom

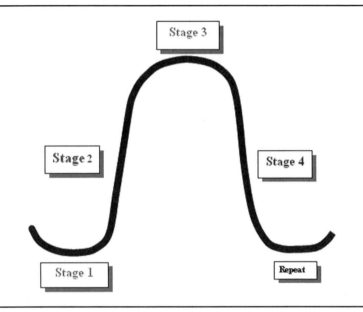

For color charts go to www.traderslibrary.com/TLEcorner

tered, you should rarely find yourself on the wrong side of any stock or market. Just in case you don't know, over 65% of all trading losses can be attributed to being on the wrong side of the stock or market.

The picture in figure 4.1 is the only motion any stock or any market is capable of making. It is a repetitive cycle, and I have labeled each stage with the number one through four. As we come back to stage one, the whole process repeats itself again. Understand also that the above smooth line is simply an average of price movement. In reality stock prices are naturally rallying and falling inside of every line. It should also be noted that it does not matter what timeframe is being represented above. This concept applies whether we're talking about a stock trading for several months, several weeks, several days, or several minutes. Let's begin on the left side of the diagram as prices are falling into what is labeled stage one.

Prices are falling as sellers are dominating the buyers. After an extended period of time the stock will begin to consolidate sideways. Why do prices stop falling after a long period of decline? It is simple, and there is only one answer. We have run out of sellers. For any stock there are a finite number of people that own the stock and there are a finite number of people that are willing to sell in any given price range. There are people that will never sell and there are people that are not ready to sell, but at any given price point a situation can be reached where we simply run out sellers.

So if we are out of sellers, why doesn't the stock immediately rally? In truth, sometimes it does. This is what we call a V bottom when it happens. It is very difficult to play a V bottom unless certain circumstances exist. More often than not, however, the stock has experienced extreme selling and at the current time, there is no one interested in purchasing the stock. Remember, this stock is then in some sort of free fall, and prudent buyers do not try to jump in and catch free falling stocks. In this situation stocks may

> Buyers create demand and sellers create supply. When demand is greater than supply, prices rise.

stay in disfavor for a long period of time. This creates a situation where there are no buyers and no sellers interested in the stock. Since no one is interested in the stock, the emotion that dominates this stage of the stock is called ambivalence. This period of time is what we call stage one and can last for a long period of time in some situations.

Eventually, if we have truly exhausted the sellers, there will be a point in time where some buyers will start shopping around. As the first buyers begin to nibble at the stock, something interesting will likely happen. The lack of sellers means that the stock price will begin to rise. Now this rally will do two things. It will first get the attention of the bulls because the stock may reach prices it has not seen in a period of time. Second it will be an opportunity for people who were long the stock to sell some of their shares.

Why would people be selling at this point in time? First, short term traders may have purchased the stock inside the stage one base and are taking profits already. Second, remember the stock re-

> The only way V bottoms and tops can be played is if they go climactic or if they are at a strong support or resistance area.

cently experienced a drastic sell-off, and while owners of the stock were not interested in selling at the stage one price, they may now be interested in getting out of the stock as the price becomes more favorable. This will setup a time where the stock begins a series of rallies and sharp pullbacks as it tries to transition its way from stage one to the next stage of the stock's life cycle.

> This is the only cycle in existence. The four stages must, and always do, occur in the same sequence.

If it is true that we have largely exhausted the supply of sellers, at this point we should see the buyers take the stock to highs that have not been seen recently. Also, they should support the stock well enough so as sellers take profits, the buyers step up to buy with enough strength that a higher low is formed. In other words, they become more and more aggressive in buying the stock on pullbacks. That is what forms higher lows. Does all this sound familiar?

> As stocks go from one stage to the next they go through a transitional period. Learning to play the transitions is the most advanced form of market play.

If that in fact happens, then we have the first two requirements of an uptrend. That then becomes the beginning of the next stage of the stocks life cycle which is stage two. This is the uptrend of the stock. The emotion that dominates stage two is the one of greed. It is a bullish time and often becomes the time of irrational exuberance. It is the time when most average people make the most money.

After a period of time in a sharp rally, the stock will begin to level off and move sideways. The reason, once again, is fairly simple. There is a finite amount of money available to a finite number of buyers, and at some point in time, we will simply run out of buyers. If we are out of buyers, why doesn't the stock immediately plummet? Sometimes it will and this is known as a V top and, like a V bottom, is very difficult to play unless a certain set of circumstances are in place. More often than not, however, the stock will not fall immediately because it is a very strong stock and there is currently no reason for holders of the stock to sell.

## What is Consolidation?

Now a quick word here about the consolidation that forms after a sharp rally. This discussion will also apply to a consolidation that follows a sharp decline. Obviously not all consolidations that follow strong moves up have immediate declines. As a matter of fact, the vast majority of times, consolidations that occur during sharp rallies or declines (stage two and stage four) are resolved in the direction of the primary trend. That is to say in this case, after a strong rally the consolidation will most likely break to the upside because the number-one rule in trading is to follow the trend.

We have a special name for a consolidation that is simply a continuation of the prior trend. It is called "a pause that refreshes." So naturally one of the key questions you will have is whether or not the consolidation after this rally will be a pause that refreshes before the stock heads higher or if it will become a stage three which will bring on lower prices.

A pause that refreshes is simply a continuation base. After the stock rests, it should continue in its prior trend.

I am going to tell you two different answers to that question. The first answer is that we don't actually need to know. We do not need to anticipate, or guess in this case, in which direction the stock will eventually head. We can wait for the stock to show which way it's going and if it resolves itself to the upside, we will continue to play the stock as we have played in the prior stage two. If it breaks to the downside, we will begin to play the stock as we will play stocks that are in stage four.

> There are three clues to help distinguish a pause from a stage three. A pause is more likely to be a tighter controlled consolidation, on decreasing volume, which stays above the rising 20-period moving average.

The second answer, as you may have guessed, is that we do have ways to help distinguish what is likely going to be a pause that refreshes or a stage that will eventually change the direction of stock. Remember that the basic swing trader can just wait until the consolidation resolves itself. This is the simplest and most accurate method for the swing trader.

Even if this is a pause that refreshes in an ongoing stage two, eventually the stock will peak out and one of these bases will be a stage three. Whenever that happens, the stock will trade below the majority of days in the prior consolidation and will not find any buyers for the first time. This will cause the stock to fall, until we see profit-taking from those who were short in the base or who shorted the breakdown. If we truly did exhaust all the buyers and this is stage three, the sellers will begin to win the battle every time

> Stocks tend to fall faster than they rally because the emotion of fear is stronger than the emotion of greed.

the stock rallies. The more this happens, the more others decide it's time to get out of the stock to either take their profits or minimize their losses. This action will continue until rallies fall short of prior rallies, and sell-offs go to new lows. This is known as stage four. It is the downtrend, and the most bearish part of the cycle, characterized by the emotion of fear.

Typically, stage four is a better money-making opportunity because stocks do tend to fall faster than they rally. I have to tell you if you are short in a true stage four, it is almost difficult to mismanage the trade.

*Knowing where you are in the cycle is your key to successful trading.*

Despite this fact, it is still true that most traders make most of their money in stage two, not stage four. This is because of the bullish bias that most traders have. Unfortunately when stage four arrives, most traders are conditioned to try to minimize losses rather than to actually make money by short selling stage four.

After a period of time, the stock will have a hard time falling further because we have run out of sellers. Now we are back to the formation of a new stage one base where we started this conversation.

FIGURE 4.2 · **The Only Way to Win or Lose**

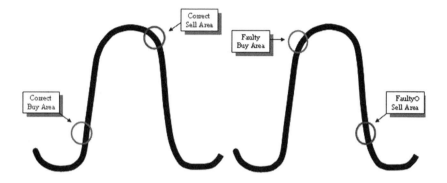

For color charts go to www.traderslibrary.com/TLEcorner

## Components of the Market's Basic Unit

Here are a few characteristics of the first of the foundational keys, the market's basic unit. First of all you must understand that this is the only complete movement a stock or the market can make. There is no other movement possible. This cycle is repeated again and again.

This cycle is comprised of four distinct stages, which in turn are ruled by four distinct emotions, and this forms the basis for one's ability to predict future price movements based on the laws of psychology and probability.

As a matter of fact, there is only one way to win and only one way to lose in the market. Take one more look at the market's basic unit in Figure 4.2.

If you are currently making money in the market, you are doing as the diagram on the left indicates in some form or fashion. There is no other way to win in the market. If you are currently not successful in the market, you are doing what is shown on the right. Regardless of whatever issues you're having, the bottom line is that you are buying and selling based on the diagram on the right, period. There is no other explanation possible.

> Successful traders make money by purchasing at the exact moment the balance of power changes and selling to the last of the buyers to get on board. There is no security in being that last buyer.

The diagram on the left shows the only way to lose. Why would anybody enter a long position so late? You may look at this and say that this could never happen to you. I challenge you to go back and look at several of your prior trades and mark your actual entries and exits on the chart. You may be very surprised by what you find. As a regular routine, my traders are required to mark up and review their charts for this very purpose. Late entries are typical, and one of our biases as human beings. We all want to be part of a crowd.

We all want security and want to be led by someone who knows at times of uncertainty. It is a sin known as a needing to know too much. With the techniques in his book, you will know precisely when to enter a stock and you will no longer need to wait to see if every other trader feels this is a good buy as well.

You may also be wondering how anyone could possibly exit a stock so late, regardless of when they entered. It does not seem possible that someone would sit through the entire decline and then decide to exit a long position. Yet this is what happens to the vast majority of traders every single day. We know statistically that most new traders do not use or will not honor a stop loss. We will be discussing the concept of entries and stops shortly, but for now I think you can see the issue presented here. There is a point in time when the stock should be exited, either due to a target being reached, a management policy, or the protective stop loss been triggered. Traders do not like to take stop losses because it makes them feel like a loser, when the truth of it is that the stop loss on losing plays is what makes a winner out of the successful traders.

You see, your job as a swing trader actually becomes quite simple. There are strategies to be used to capture gains in each of the four stages that any stock or market goes through. The key to trading successfully is knowing where you are in the cycle.

# Self-test questions

1. In technical terms (given no changes in fundamentals or unusual news events), why will a strong stock drop?

   a. Overbought—Indicators signal overbought and traders sell

   b. Emotions—Fear of the upcoming reversal causes a reversal

   c. Supply and demand—Buyers have all bought and there are none left; the stock can only go down

   d. Cycles—Stocks are seasonal and tend to rise and fall in yearly cycles

2. After a sell-off, why is an immediate rise in the stock, creating a V-shaped chart pattern, unlikely?

   a. It should enter a stage 1 cycle of "ambivalence" and go sideways

   b. It needs a pause that refreshes before going anywhere

   c. It should experience a "dead cat bounce" before continuing to drop

   d. Such "fallen" stocks attract no trader interest and continue to go down

3. At what stage do most traders make money in the market?

   a. Transitional Stage 1 periods—they can almost guaranteed not to lose money
   b. Stage 2 uptrend—"irrational exuberance"
   c. Stage 4 downtrend—fastest mover
   d. Stage 3—top of the cycle means top dollar

4. What are the characteristics of a "pause that refreshes"?

   a. It doesn't break the trendline established by the 20-period moving average
   b. Indicators show a trend reversal
   c. A lack of interest in the stock by both buyers and sellers
   d. Bowl-shaped chart pattern

5. According to Velez, what is the key to successful trading?

   a. Hard work and patience
   b. Knowing where you are in the 4-stage cycle
   c. Mastering shorting the market
   d. Astute, aggressive high-volume trading

**For answers, go to www.traderslibrary.com/TLEcorner**

# Chapter 5

# The Market's Three Directions

## The Movement of Stocks

This brings me to the second of our foundational blocks. It may sound very simple, but I will show you in very short order how powerful this very simple concept is.

There are only three things a stock can do: go up, go down, or go sideways. That's it. There is no other movement possible. In other words there are primarily three dominant trends in the market: uptrends, downtrends, and sideways trends.

An uptrend is defined as follows:

1. A series of higher highs and a series of higher lows on the rallies. In other words, each successive rally takes out or su-

persedes the prior peak from the prior rally. Each drop holds above the low of the prior drop.

2. A rising 20- and a rising 40-period moving average. We use simple moving averages based on the close.

3. The rising 20- and 40-period moving averages have a consistent distance between them. We call that a "railroad track" appearance. When you have this picture, you have a stock in an uptrend that is completely dominated by the buyers. See Figure 5.1.

---

## FIGURE 5.1 - Pristine Uptrend Defined

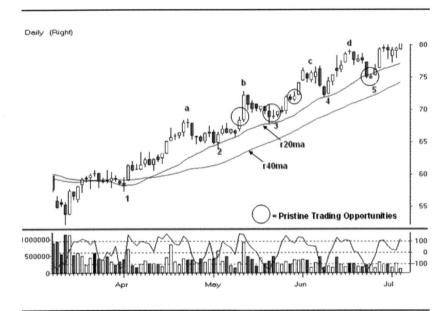

Daily (Right)

= Pristine Trading Opportunities

For color charts go to www.traderslibrary.com/TLEcorner

---

I want you to keep the definition in mind because it's going to become very important as we move forward. As a matter of fact the quality of your long trades will vary directly with the quality of the uptrend that the stock is in.

The definition of a downtrend is just the reverse:

1. A series of lower highs and a series of lower on the sell-offs. In other words, each successive drop takes out or falls below the prior low from the prior decline. Each counter rally falls far short of the high of the prior rally.

2. A declining 20- and a declining 40-period moving average, using simple moving averages based on the close.

3. The declining 20- and 40-period moving averages have a consistent distance between them. We call that a "railroad track" appearance. When you have this picture, you have a stock in a downtrend that is completely dominated by the sellers.

The stock in Figure 5.2 is an example of a downtrend. I want to take a moment to discuss the difference psychologically between uptrends and downtrends. There is a tremendous bias among Americans and new traders especially to be bullish on the stock market. It is important for you to understand that you cannot carry a preconceived bias into the market. You must be willing to adapt and be bullish or bearish depending upon the trend of the timeframe you are playing.

## FIGURE 5.2 - Pristine Downtrend Defined

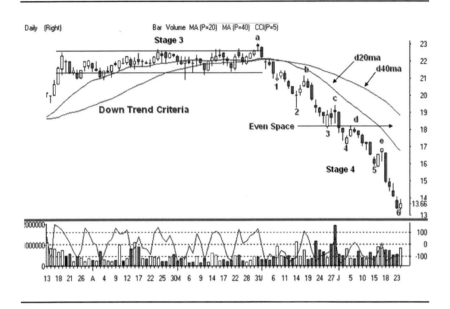

This can be a difficult task for many people, and many people struggle to understand downtrends or bearish strategies. In every case, without exception, the strategy to short a stock is exactly the reverse of the strategy to be long a stock. The decision of which direction to favor must be based totally and impartially on the trend of the chart you are playing.

Third, we have the sideways trend. The sideways trend is defined as a stock having relatively equal highs and relatively equal lows.

FIGURE 5.3 - Sideways Trend Defined

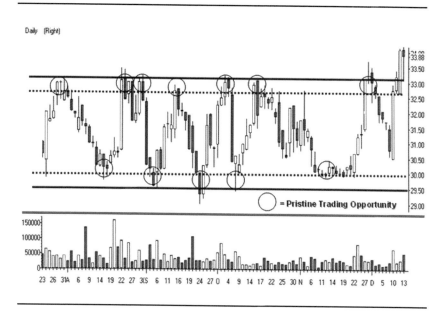

There is a tug-of-war going on between both groups and neither of the groups is winning. See Figure 5.3.

The keyword in that definition is "relatively" equal highs and lows. It is important to understand that these areas of highs and lows are being formed by support and resistance areas. They have to be considered fairly wide areas. We do not react to exact price points, but rather turning points that have been in the area of support and resistance.

The terminology for buying and shorting stocks is as follows: When you want to buy a stock and capture an upward movement, you open the position by "buying" the stock and you close the position by "selling" the stock. When you want to short sell a stock and capture a downward movement, you open the position by "shorting" the stock and you close the position by "covering" the stock.

## Playing the Trend

So, there are only three trends. The uptrend, downtrend, and sideways trend. These three trends make up every single movement in the market. There are only three. If I can teach you how to play with a great degree of accuracy each one of these three trends, I can teach you how to cover yourself in every possible market environment in existence.

If you find a stock that is making a series of higher highs and higher lows, that means that you are in an uptrend. This is the bullish part of the stocks cycle where greed will continue to rally the stock. This is stage two, and your action as a swing trader is to buy the very next decline. I want you to understand this because it is critical. If you find a stock that strictly meets the criteria of the definition of an uptrend, higher highs and higher lows, your job as a swing trader is to buy every single decline; not some of them, not a few of them, but every single one. The only question you have to answer is when. Not if. When. We will discuss when and how to buy them shortly.

If you find a stock that is making a series of lower highs and lower lows, you obviously are in a downtrend. This is the most bearish time of the stocks cycle known as stage four. It is led by the emotion of fear, and fear will dominate the action until the downtrend ends. If you are in a downtrend, your action is to short every single rally and consolidation breakdown. I am telling you that I don't care what the earnings report says. I don't care what some high paid Wall Street analyst with frayed shirtsleeves say. The rallies that occur in this stock are nothing to get excited about. As a matter of fact, every single rally is a sellable rally until the downtrending pattern ends.

If you are in a sideways trend, meaning relatively equal highs and relatively equal lows, you, as a market player, can play both. You can buy the declines and you can sell the rallies. We will discuss how to buy and sell these shortly.

There are many names given to sideways trends. You may have heard terms such as channels, consolidations, shelves, or any of a dozen different names. However, in truth, there are only three types of sideways trends in the market's basic unit. That sideways trend is either a stage one, a stage three, or a pause that refreshes. You will never confuse a stage one with a stage three if you understand the life cycle

> All sideways trends have to be either a stage one, a stage three, or a pause that refreshes. There are no other choices.

of the stock. Stage three can only follow stage two and stage one can only follow stage four. As I discussed above the only issue will be distinguishing a pause that refreshes from a stage one or from a stage three. However, regardless of which of the three sideways trends the stock is in, the base can be shorted at the top, and the bottom of the base can be bought until the sideways trend ends.

## The Importance of Knowing When to React

Now this may sound very basic to you, but this very simple concept gives you the ability to perform better than 98% of the so-called professionals out there, or the talking heads on television programs like CNBC. The $64,000 question every single day in the market is how do I know when a decline is an opportunity, or when a decline is a reason for me to run for the hills? Isn't that the prevailing question? Aren't entire television shows dedicated to that one answer?

One guy says you should buy because the stock is going higher; another guy says no; the stock is completely shot, there is no more momentum. The two guys are battling on this one question. Is the decline in the stock an opportunity to buy or is it the first sign of trouble?

This concept answers the question. If the stock has made a new high and the decline is falling from a new high, that decline is buyable. It is not a reason to take flight. It is not a reason to get nervous. It is a buyable decline. The same is true in reverse.

FIGURE 5.4 - The Mighty r20ma

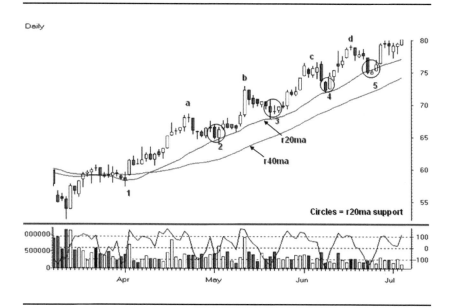

Daily

For color charts go to www.traderslibrary.com/TLEcorner

With this one simple, basic concept you now have the ability to hold your very own CNBC buy, hold, or sell session. Imagine taking your first call and John from Wichita says, "My broker says I should buy WXYZ. Do I buy it, sell it, or hold it?" And you could say, "Well, sir; I've just taken a quick look at the daily chart of WXYZ and I see a very powerful series of higher highs and higher lows. Each time the stock rallies, it is strong enough to take out the peak from the prior rally. Each time it drops, the sellers are incap-

FIGURE 5.5 - Downtrend Begins

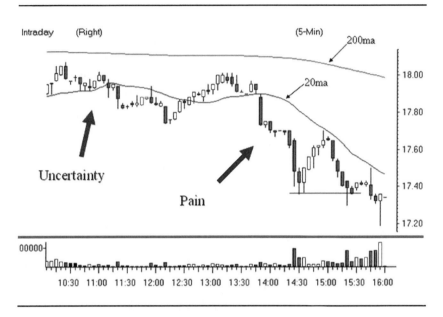

Intraday    (Right)                                    (5-Min)

For color charts go to www.traderslibrary.com/TLEcorner

able of bringing it as low as they did the last time. This is in fact a very strong stock. So your job then, John from Wichita, is to buy on the very next decline."

Another individual can call up after you've been thanked by John and say, "You know what? My broker says that I should be buying ABC." And you say, "Well, ma'am; I have just taken a look at the daily chart of ABC, and the first thing I want you to do is to fire your broker." That is because this stock is in a severe downtrend. Every single time it rallies, it's a feeble rally that is incapable of coming anywhere near the prior top and every time the sellers take it down they take it down deeper and further. This stock is being dominated by the sellers. And I suggest that if you happen to have bought already, that on the very next rally you get out. If you haven't bought, stay away from the stock until that pattern changes.

Figure 5.4 is the picture of the uptrend. It is the picture of greed leading every rally to higher highs and every pullback finding a higher low. It is smooth, steady, and consistent. The bulls are in control of the entire process.

Figure 5.5 is the picture of pain. Can you hear them? First, the sideways trend is showing the picture of uncertainty and/or ambivalence. Then the uncertainty becomes fear as prices begin falling, which causes prices to fall faster and pure pain sets in. Soon, more and more will sell until there are no sellers left. Prices will stabilize, but no one will really care where the stock is heading next.

## As the World Turns

This cycle is the same every time. Extreme fear causes extreme selling until sellers run out. Then a period of ambivalence while everyone ignores the stock, followed by the realization that the sellers are gone, and the stock begins to move up. The buying continues until pure greed takes over. Prices accelerate until no one is certain if the stock can continue any higher, so it stalls during the period of uncertainty. This happens over and over and over again.

# Self-test questions

1. What is a characteristic of an uptrend?

   a. The 20- and 40-period moving averages crisscrossing each other
   b. +100 CCI reading
   c. Rising volume
   d. Railroad track appearance of the 20- and 40-period moving averages

2. What is the difference in trading an uptrend versus a downtrend?

   a. Uptrends are easier to trade
   b. More corrective counter-rallies in downtrends
   c. Downtrends tend to be faster
   d. CCI is more reliable in a downtrend

3. What defines a sideways trend?

   a. Indicators giving contradictory or mixed signals
   b. Relatively equal highs and lows
   c. A stock bouncing off of support
   d. A stock in "pause" mode

4. When are optimal times to short a stock?

   a. When a stock in an uptrend breaks below the 20-period moving average
   b. In an uptrend when the stock reverses from a higher high
   c. During a stage 3 consolidation, when the stock reaches the low point
   d. In a downtrend when a stock manages to break its lowest low

5. The benefits of the Pristine system are that it eliminates

   a. The majority of trading opportunities, to guarantee only a few winning trades
   b. Daytrading intraday chart patterns
   c. Relying on the fear and greed of others to make money
   d. Listening and relying on market news and analysts

6. How do I cover a stock?

   a. Sell a stock to exit a position
   b. Buy an equal stake in an opposite position
   c. Buy a stock to exit a short position
   d. Pay in cash

For answers, go to www.traderslibrary.com/TLEcorner

# Chapter 6

# The Buy and Sell Setup

## Know Exactly How to Play the Market Trend

We now know the two foundational keys; the market's basic unit and the only three trends in existence. Based on this concept, I have identified the instances in which we want to buy or to short the stock. Once we're in a well-defined uptrend known as stage two, all pullbacks are buyable. Once we're in a well-defined downtrend known as stage four, all rallies are shortable. If we are in a sideways trend known as stage one, stage three, or a pause that refreshes, we know that the bottom of the consolidation is buyable and the top of the consolidation shortable. The question we have now to answer is HOW do we buy or short and exactly where. To answer this question we use the buy and sell setup.

## The Buy and Sell Setup in an Uptrend

Let's begin discussing how to use the Buy Setup when the stock is in the uptrend, or stage two. Remember that it is a requirement of our uptrend that the stock makes a new recent high. When we talk about making new highs, we do not mean new all-time highs or 52-week highs or even one month highs. We simply mean a high that was able to exceed the last rally's high. Once this happens, the stock will inevitably begin some sort of pullback. This is when we begin watching the stock for the appropriate setup.

FIGURE 6.1 - Anatomy of an Uptrend

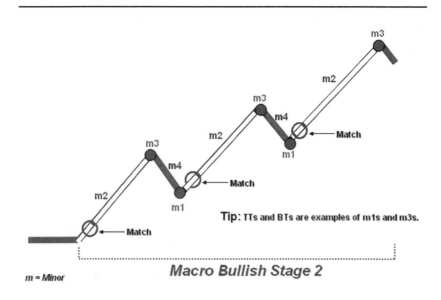

For color charts go to www.traderslibrary.com/TLEcorner

I want you to notice something at this point. When a stock is in stage two, it is making higher highs on the rallies and higher lows on the pullbacks. We often refer to this as the macro stage two. The rallies and pullbacks that occur inside of the macro stage two are in fact small rallies, consolidations, and pullbacks that are really stages one, two, three, and four in the micro sense. Look at the diagram in Figure 6.1.

## Watch for the Pullbacks

The big picture of this stock is that it is moving up higher highs and higher lows. However, inside this macro stage two, the individual rallies are micro stage twos. The pullbacks are micro stage fours, and the periods of time in between are stages one and three. On the micro timeframe, stages one and three can be reversals or single moments in time. They may be comprised simply of a topping or bottoming tail, a narrow bar, a change in the color of the bar (white-white-white-black) or a gap up or down.

When the stock is in a macro stage two and a micro stage two, we are simply watching and waiting. As the micro stage goes to stage three, we continue to watch. Remember, this is stage three on this micro level after the rally to new highs. We then watch as micro stage four takes this stock on its first pullback of this new rally. If the stock is going to continue its uptrend, the micro stage four will find buyers before trading under prior micro stage four and start micro stage one. Now remember, stage one could simply be a bottoming tail, or a narrow bar, or a white bar after all blacks, or a gap up. During micro stage one we're getting ready to strike. As micro stage two emerges inside of the macro stage two, this is when we strike.

The process of monitoring the pullback, which is the micro stage four, and how this becomes a stage one and stage two is what we want to look at now and is what comprises the Buy Setup.

There should be some light bulbs going on as you read this last paragraph. If not, read the prior section until you fully understand the significance. The key to successful trading is to make sure that we have a stage to stage match. In other words, when we are in macro stage two, we only want to be buying, and buying only when micro stage two begins. The exact reverse is also true for being short. When in macro stage four, we want to short, and short only when micro stage four begins. This stage to stage match is a priceless concept and at the heart of every swing trade.

## Focus in on Pullbacks

Let's take a look at the pullback that makes up the stage four inside the macro stage two. In order to form the buy setup, we need the pullback to occur over three or more days. To qualify as a pullback day, we need the stock to either have a black bar or a lower high than the prior day. It would be nice to have both, and it would also be nice to have a lower low than the prior day as well. However, only a black bar or a lower high is required. So to meet the requirements of the buy setup, the stock must put in either three lower highs or 3 black bars.

After a new high, I want to see pain last for at least three days. If you have made a new high, all you have to do is wait in the wings for at least three days. Then step back up to the plate and find someone who has sat through pain for three or more days. You say, "Sir, is there something wrong? Can I help you? Is that stock causing you trouble? I'll take that. I'll take it all, by the way, and no, there is no need to thank me."

What happens is that someone who bought at the high has now sat through pain. Day one they had a headache; day two they had a migraine; day three they cried on their spouse's shoulder; day four they just simply could not take it anymore, called up their broker or pressed the sell button. They said, "get this piece of junk out of my life."

Once I have three or more lower highs or black bars (or both, or three lower lows also), ideally what I also would like to have is three or more consecutive bars where the stock opens near the high of the day and closes near the low of the day. Three nice solid black bars. What does that tell me? That tells me that the sellers have created pain, solid pain, for three steady days. There was no break in the pain. None. They do not give them even a brief moment to breathe a sigh of relief. I want the pain to be severe.

Now we're set to strike. The action will be to buy the stock as soon as it trades above the prior day's high. This is the sign of strength we need to begin stage two in the micro timeframe and to show the stock is ready to continue stage two on the macro timeframe. However, just knowing when to buy the stock is not enough.

## Remember the Four Parts of Every Trade

There are four parts to every trade. I need to know the entry price, the stop loss price, the target area, and how to manage the trade from the entry and my target. We have just determined the entry price. Let's talk a little bit about each of the other parts of the trade.

## The Entry

First let's talk more about the entry. We know the entry will be made above the prior bar's high once our setup is in place. This is the standard entry. There is a circumstance that can occur where we can use an alternate entry, if you have the capability of being with a market in the morning. If you are trading remotely, this may not be a choice. This circumstance occurs when the last bar down is a very wide bar. The problem is that entry over this bar will cause the stop loss to be very far away. It may be far enough away that you no longer desire to take the trade. If this is the case, we can substitute a 30 minute high entry on the current day rather than waiting to trade over the prior day's high. This means that you let the stock trade for 30 minutes, mark off a high of the day at that time, and buy the stock when it trades over that 30 minute high. You will be getting in before the prior days high in this case, so the failure rate will be higher when you opt for this technique. The advantage is that your stop will be much smaller and in some cases, it may be the only option other than passing the trade.

> In some cases, a 30-minute high of the current day can be used to enter the stock.

While we're talking about entries, let's discuss what to do if the stock actually opens above the prior day's high. This is called gapping up. It means that the stock opens the trading day at a price higher than it closed the prior day. This can happen because of news that affects the market in general or news about the specific stock. When this happens, you need to make a decision about whether the gap is excessive or not. As a guideline I like to say that a gap of 50¢ or more for the average $30 stock is excessive. Anything less than that is not. If there is a gap up that is not excessive, you may simply buy the stock because it has now triggered above the prior day's high. If the gap is excessive, you use the thirty-minute buy rule. This means that we let the stock trade for 30 minutes and only buy if it is strong enough to take out its 30 minute high.

The reason for this rule is that stocks may gap up excessively only to trade down the rest of the day. There is no point in entering a stock when it stays weak all day.

> If the stock gaps up excessively, use the 30-minute buy rule to be safe.

## The Stop Loss

Next let's talk about stop losses. A protective stop loss is known as an insurance policy because it protects against the catastrophic loss of hanging on to a losing trade with no action plan in place. A trade should never be entered without knowing 1) where the stop loss is and 2) making sure that the trade is exited if the stop loss is hit. For the buy setup, we will always be placing the stop underneath the entry bar or the prior bar, whichever is lower.

Some traders will add a few pennies to the entry price and subtract a few pennies from the stop loss price to avoid "false triggers" where the stock trades above or below the number you are watching but never follows through.

You see, every market player needs to draw a line in the sand. You need to mark off a point at which you are not willing to go beyond. The ostrich approach in the market does not work. We need to draw a line that says if the stock does not perform, and it hits this line, it gets eliminated. Every single stock I buy, I look at as my employee. It either has to perform or it gets fired. And that line is basically telling the stock "You touch this line, and you're out of my life" and you move on to the next trade.

I need to stop here and comment for a moment on the use of protective stop losses. It is a fact that the vast majority of traders who fail to generate profits trading, whether they be long-term or short-term, do so because of the failure to follow stop losses. Now

I just gave you the formula for where to place a protective stop loss. It goes under the current entry bar or the prior bar, whichever bar is lower. That is not difficult to understand. So you need to realize that the traders who do not follow stop losses do not do so because they cannot figure out where to place a stop loss. There are psychological demons that set into virtually everybody when they trade, and these demons often prohibit people from actually stopping the trade even though they know exactly where to stop it.

Here is a situation where you may use an altered stop. If the distance to the low of the prior bar is so wide that once again the stop becomes prohibitively large, you may opt to use the current days low even though it is not the lower of the two.

## The Target

Now let's take a look at the target. If you have noticed, we have determined an entry and stop loss price that will literally be to the penny. Targets are a little trickier, however. We know that if we are in an uptrend, we can expect to meet or exceed the prior high. Therefore, this will always be our first goal for a target area. The problem is that in strong uptrends, many times the stock may go

> The distance from my entry price to my target, compared to the distance from my entry price to the stop, is known as the reward to risk ratio. Many traders set up a minimum reward to risk ratio before taking a trade.

far beyond that prior high. It is not very satisfying to be out of a trade while it runs several times beyond your intended target.

Taking targets is one of my worst demons. For a long time I was always too quick to take profits only to see a large chunk of the trade sit on the table as the stock rallied without me. That is why I've become a firm believer in incremental target taking. What that means quite simply is setting multiple targets in the general areas the stock may be likely to run and to manage them on the way up. This allows me to "take home some bacon today" while still leaving some of the trade on for the big move.

Another idea I like to use is to trail stop the last part of a trade. This will become clearer as I discuss management in the next paragraph; but, the idea is to let part of the trade continue to rally for as long as the stock does.

## Managing The Trade

Finally we need to discuss the management of the trade. This is pretty straightforward, but there are a couple of options that are available. When I first enter the trade, I have my initial stop loss in place. This is where I will exit the stock if it does not move in my favor. I will keep this stop in place for the first two days; meaning, the day that I enter the stock as well as day two. Then on day three I will raise that stop to the low of day two. On day four the stop will become the low of day three, and so on. This is known as a "bar by bar" trail stop because every prior bar's low becomes your new stop.

Note that this policy does not begin until day three. For the first two days of the trade, the original stop is used.

I use the original stop for two days initially because sometimes the trade may be slow to get moving. Here is where another option may come in to play. Everyone has a different level of patience and tolerance and this may affect how you wish to manage some of the finer points of these trades. If you like to give the stock a little more room while adhering to the original stop, you may want to consider keeping the original stop in place beyond the recommended two days. Wait until the stock price travels more than halfway to the first target before you begin a bar by bar trail stop management policy. Sometimes getting the stop too tight, too early in the trade, is not beneficial. Give the stock some room to get going and once it shows that it is moving up, then use the bar by bar trail stop.

In Figure 6.2 we can review the buy setup. Let's assume the four white bars have just made a new recent high in a stage two uptrend. We now begin the pullback. The first black bar is also the first lower high. The second black bar is the second lower high and the third black bar is also the third lower high. We only have two lower lows at this point, but remember, that is optional. This means that at this point in time, after three black bars, this stock could be purchased at point A over the high of the third black bar. You could either place a buy stop order with your broker that morning, or set an alarm for that price if you are going to be with the market all day.

FIGURE 6.2 - Buy Setup

# The Setup | The Action

**Main Criterion:**    **3 or more consecutive lower highs _or_**
**3 or more black bars.**
*Tip: Having both makes the set-up more potent.*

**Optional Item:**    **3 or more consecutive lower lows**

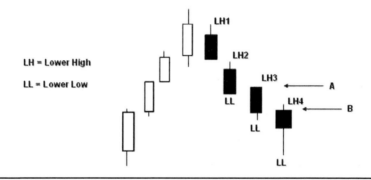

LH = Lower High

LL = Lower Low

For color charts go to www.traderslibrary.com/TLEcorner

Notice that while the stock was eligible to be purchased this day, it did not trigger. That is to say the stock never traded over the prior day's high. Should we throw this out of our watchlist now? Of course not. We are going to continue to monitor it the next day and continue this process every day until it is no longer making a higher low. The next day a fourth black bar appears, giving us four

If you are not available during market hours, automatic entries and exits can be placed with your broker to execute a trade when you are not even there. They are called stop orders.

FIGURE 6.3 - PBS Four Action Steps

The Setup | **The Action**

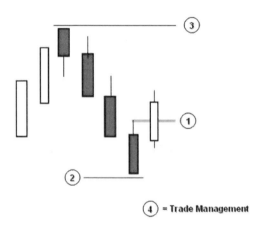

④ = Trade Management

black bars with four lower highs and three lower lows. The stock can now be bought over the last black bar or at point B.

Figure 6.3 shows us the action once the stock trades over the prior bar's high. Remember the four parts to every trade?

1. Enter over the prior day's high (remember you may use a 30 minute high if the prior day has a very wide bar);

2. Place a protective stop loss under today's low or yesterday's low, whichever is lower;

3. Set your first target for the prior high from the last rally. Remember in an uptrend you should easily exceed this, but this is a minimum target;

4. Once a trade is entered go into management mode. Let the stock trade for two days without changing the stop (minimum) and then switch to a bar by bar trail stop or your own personal management plan.

Figure 6.4 is a sample of this strategy at work using Chase Manhattan Bank. What we have on the far left of the chart is a rally to make a new high. Once the stock has made a new high, I am

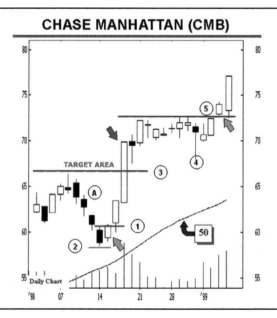

waiting for three or more consecutive lower highs or three black bars. That's my only strict criteria. I'd like to have both and I'd like to have three lower lows also, but I don't have to have that.

Now the stock experiences one lower high, two lower highs, three lower highs. I've got my three; now I start tracking the highs. My buy is on the next day if in fact it manages to trade above that high. CMB needed four lower highs or five black bars before it traded over the prior day's high. Once in, I am placing my protective stop below the current bar's low, or the prior bar's low, whichever is lower. In this case it is the prior bar's low. I've got my insurance policy in place and I know my target areas.

Now, let's discuss profit-taking. If we are dealing with stocks that are making higher highs and higher lows, and the prior high is four dollars away, what is the minimum profit objective you come up with? Four dollars. That is because if we are in fact playing an uptrend, the odds suggest that the next swing will break above the prior high. So my prior high serves as my minimum profit objective. A minimum.

Once the stock takes out that prior high quite nicely, I flip into sell mode. The public is taught to buy new highs. The professional is taught to sell new highs. The professional needs a rush of amateurs coming in on new highs so that they can get out on new highs and then step back and get back in line and wait for pain to start the process again.

This is the professional approach. This strategy forces you to come in right at the end of the cycle called pain, and it forces you to exit right near the high of the cycle called greed. You see, we want to sell when it becomes obvious to the world that this stock is now strong. We want to buy when it's not obvious to a great many people that the stock has finished its period of pain.

Isn't it possible for me to leave a lot of money on the table? Absolutely it is. It doesn't sound logical, but the more professional your trading becomes, the more money you will leave on the table.

## Know When to Take Your Profit

You see, novices are the only ones that can truly speak of grabbing huge moves in a single score. Professionals think like this; one out of every ten trades will rally ten dollars or more. Let's just use that as an arbitrary number. One in every ten of your trades will rally ten dollars. Let's say three in every ten trades will rally four dollars. Let's say seven in every ten trades will rally two dollars. Let's say nine trades in every ten will rally seventy-five cents. What do you think the professional will do? He will take the nine wins out of every ten trades every single time because all he has to do to make up the difference is increase his share size. The professional will go for accuracy over the gamble because he does not know, of the nine trades in the first scenario, which won't work, or whether one or two or three of them will open down twenty dollars. He does not know how much he's going to lose on the nine trades. But, he does know that under the latter scenario, he can win nine times out of ten. Once he has the winning record, he has two things he needs to do; increase the size and increase the frequency of activity. This is a far more professional approach.

I have stopped fighting my number one problem as a trader. My fault as a trader is that I take profits too soon. I love to ring the cash register. And part of that was built into me simply because when I first started in this business, I either made money or I didn't eat. So when I had money on the table and I was hungry, I had to take the money off the table. This has been engrained in me and I struggle with this problem to this very day. I leave zillions of dollars on the table because I take profits quite quickly. For years I battled and tried to conquer this problem. What is interesting is that there was a constant battle between two demons; one demon would sit on my left shoulder, the other demon would sit on my right shoulder. The one demon on my left shoulder would say, "You know you always do this. You've got a little tiny profit in your hands and here is going to be another time you're going take it too soon and the stock's going to rock."

So I say, "Yeah, you know what? That's right." Then the other demon says, "No, do you remember the last time you tried to hold on for a bigger profit? You did it at the wrong time and what happened? You lost big, right?"

There is that constant battle between these two sides and invariably when I decided that I'm going to go for the bigger gain; that was the time not to go for the bigger gain.

> Incremental selling allows you to take home some money immediately while also letting you stay with the trade for the bigger move and the bigger money.

So I've helped solve part of this problem by doing the following. Instead of trying to pick one demon over the other, I realized that both demons are with me forever, so I try to make friends with both of them. I say, "You know what? Instead of trying to satisfy one over the other, I'm going to satisfy both of you. I am going to take some now, so now get off my left shoulder. Then I am going to keep some for a bigger gain. Now you get off of my right shoulder." This created the concept of what we call the incremental sell. I am not smart enough, even after all my years of trading, to know where the top is. So what I do is buy and sell in parts. I may buy one lot, but sell in three parts. In other words, once the stock breaks above to a new high, I sell one third. If it goes higher, I then dish out another third. It continues to go higher, I dish out another third.

Remember, as the stock moves higher I am getting closer to what? I am getting closer to that individual who buys and can't find another buyer. So I do not want to be stuck at the top and be that individual with all of my merchandise. If I do get stuck with that individual, I want most of my merchandise to have already been sold, and I only want to be stuck with the smaller amount. So once the stock breaks into a new high, I sell incrementally.

On the second rally we make a brand new high. Once it makes a high, I step back. I'm out of the stock already. No pain experienced by the way. I have not sat through three days of the stock not doing anything; I have not sat through three days of the stock going in the opposite direction. I have captured a pocket of time in the stock, a sweet spot, and got off before any pain set in.

Now I'm walking right down to the bottom floor again and waiting for the stock to come to me. The next time it experiences three or more consecutive lower highs, I'm right back in there tracking highs. Sometimes it is so strong that there are buyers available to compensate for all of the selling and profit-taking that takes place. If this happens, the stock will often go sideways for a period of time. This is known as a time correction rather than the price correction. Once the stock breaks over the high of the consolidation, it may be bought as a breakout. It is at arrow number two that this happens. Once I'm in, I place a stop below the current bar's low or the prior bar's low, whichever is lower and viola. Once the stock moves to a new daily high or once it breaks above the prior high, I am ready to sell in parts.

What you should do is come up with your own system. With every extra dollar, you can sell another part of the trade. Or every extra two dollars, sell another. Remember, though, to never let it drop below your entry price once you approach that first target.

> A correction through time may lead to a different entry strategy
> known as a break out.

You can also use a trailing stop method, meaning that once you sell some, you can place a stop under the low of the prior bar. Let's say it's Thursday. Your stop is under Wednesday's low. It's now Friday; it's under Thursday's low. It's Monday; it's under Friday's low. And so forth and so on until the stock takes you out. Or until the stock experiences what I call a novice gap.

A novice gap is a stock that gaps up significantly higher than the prior night's close after the stock has already run for three, four, five days in a row. That is a novice gap; a gap that is basically being created and driven by people who do not know what they're doing. People who buy at thirty.

> Novice gaps are caused by the group of traders who wait until the
> stock has moved up significantly before deciding to buy. The gap up
> is often caused by good news of some kind, but the novice trader
> doesn't understand that the price has already moved up to encom-
> pass the news.

A lot of times, we are buying because this drop is a temporary period of pain. Market makers and specialists are squeezing shares out of the hands of weak holders and then they're gobbling it all back at this point and ramming the stock back to the upside. We are jumping on board the stock the moment, the instant, fear and uncertainty turn to greed.

# Self-test questions

1.  In a stage 4 downtrend, when do you short a stock?

    a.  In a micro stage 2
    b.  In a macro stage 1
    c.  When micro stage 4 begins
    d.  You should already be short a stage 4 stock

2.  Under which of the following circumstances is the Pristine buy signal given?

    a.  After experiencing three agonizing days of pain
    b.  After three big, black down bars
    c.  After 3 big, black down bars (three agonizing days of pain), followed by the first white bar candlestick
    d.  Following 3 black bars, when the stock trades above the prior day's high

3.  Where would your stop-loss go if a stock gaps higher on opening—say 25 cents on a $20 stock?

    a.  At the low of the first 30 minutes of trading
    b.  At the low of the previous day
    c.  At the opening price, assuming the stock rises after gapping up
    d.  At the high of the previous day (low of the gap)

4. Which is an exception to the Pristine stop-loss rule (sell at today's low or yesterday's low, whichever is lower)?

   a. If the previous day's low is from a large bar day and the low gives a bad risk/reward ratio
   b. If you've had a series of losses and statistically shouldn't have another loss
   c. If a stock enters a pause that refreshes, you can discontinue the stop-loss
   d. To avoid being whipsawed from a position

5. To think like a professional trader, you need to

   a. Visualize huge gains
   b. Buy as the stock reaches new highs
   c. Ride the winners
   d. Go for small percentage gains on high percentage plays

6. Which of the four steps in the Pristine method is the most flexible?

   a. Entry point
   b. Protective stop-loss
   c. Target
   d. Management mode

**For answers, go to www.traderslibrary.com/TLEcorner**

# Chapter 7

# The Technology of Stock Trading

Swing trading involves doing your homework every night and coming to the market in the morning with a list of stocks, each having a potential buy price or short sell price. How do you go about finding this list of stocks? There are a couple of different methods.

You may want to rely on a computerized scan that will automatically pick out the setups you are looking for. To find something like a Pristine Buy Setup, you would have to become very familiar with a scanning package to enter the parameters needed to find a Pristine Buy Setup. I use Pristine's ESP™, which eliminates the need to program anything yourself. Pristine ESP™ is a scanning software that already has all the parameters built in for all of the Pristine setups. There are dozens and dozens of tactics built-in that go well beyond setups you are learning in this book. To use Pristine's

ESP™, you simply go to the swing trading scans and pull up one of the different lists for Pristine buy and sell setups. A list of stocks will pop into your charting package that contains stocks that have met the requirements I have described in this book.

> Computerized scans such as Pristine's ESP™ can help shorten your preparation time.

If you are going to scan a list of stocks manually to find the setups, you will first need to develop your own personal universe of stocks. There are thousands of stocks in the market, and you simply do not have time to go through that many stocks one by one. Many of these are penny-stocks, or trade with such light volume that you would never trade them. So your job in creating your own personal universe is to develop a list of stocks that contains a number of stocks you feel comfortable having in your list to scan every night.

You may create this list by combining several lists of stocks that you like, such as the Dow 30, the NASDAQ 100, and the semi-conductor stocks. Another way to create the list would be to filter out everything you don't want to see, such as stocks that are priced under a certain dollar amount, or stocks that trade under a certain volume. These numbers will be different for every trader because everyone has different account sizes and different share sizes they are willing to purchase to hold overnight. Another method of creating your own personal universe is to simply use one of the built-in universes that can be found in the Pristine's ESP™.

Your job is then to go through your universe every night and look for what I have described in this book. This is where the length of your list will have to vary with the time you have available to spend scanning.

Another method involves only about one hour on the weekend and a few minutes each day to develop your swing trading lists. Here is what I like to do. Over the weekend I go through my trading universe. As I go through every stock, I am looking for only two things; uptrending stocks and downtrending stocks. The ones I find that have met the requirements for uptrends and downtrends as I have described in his book, I pull out and put on a separate watchlist. Then every evening I go through my uptrend list, and what do you think I look for? That's right, three black bars or three lower highs. Likewise I go through my downtrend list and look for three white bars or three higher lows.

> A simple yet very affective method for daily swing trading can involve as little as one hour on the weekend and a few minutes every evening.

When I find these, they go on my hot list for the next day. On this list of stocks you place alerts right at yesterday's high or low and you wait. You let the market come to you. You have mapped out the plan. You have set the rules for the market and when the market plays by your rules, there is not a moment's hesitation.

The moment, the instant an alert goes off, you hit it, place your protective stop, and sit back and let magic work. This is playing the market. The problem with most individuals is that they let the market play them. If the market does not fall within your plan, you sit and read the paper.

I also want to talk to you about power trading combos. The information you have learned in his book is priceless and can lead the way to profitable trading. However, it would be the height of naivety to for anyone to think that mastery of the stock market can come from reading a book. There are many things that go into being a successful trader. There are even additional things that can be learned about the strategies in this book. For example, there are over 10 combos that can be added to the setups you have learned. They can increase the accuracy and profitability of these trades by a great deal. It is beyond the scope of this course book to go through all of them, but I would like to show you one so you can appreciate the power that these combos can bring to your existing strategies.

## Looking for the Patterns

The idea of combos is simple. I want to find one specific event that happens with a high degree of accuracy over and over and over again. You will find many instances of the Pristine Buy Setup when you scan. The idea is to combine that with other events that actually strengthen the reliability.

Let's take a look at an example of one of these combos. The combos come into play when the stock is on that three or more bar pullback from the new high. These combos enhance the quality and or profitability as the stock is getting ready to move back into its micro stage two. I am going to show you what we call a narrow range day or a narrow range bar.

The concept of a narrow range bar is not something that I can put a number on. It is a concept that is measured entirely in a visual way, but the narrow range bar is only significant when it appears after a several day move in one direction. The distance between the high of the bar and the low of the bar is smaller than the last four to five trading sessions. Here is what it looks like.

Figure 7.1 is showing you the Pristine Buy Setup with the next day being added as a narrow range bar. It does not matter if it is black or white and is also acceptable if it is a narrow body only, with tails on the top and bottom. These four examples are in the middle pane of Figure 7.1.

This example shows four days of pain in the micro stage four. This is the pullback that is setting up our Pristine Buy Setup. After four days of pain, a very small bar has formed. The small bar is showing a slowing of momentum. In other words, the bears were in control for the last four days, but can no longer push the stock down as they used to. That is how a narrow range bar forms. That is significant. When a narrow range bar forms after a several day move to the downside, it is the sign that the stocks should be ready to turn back to the upside.

On the reverse side, if the stock has experienced three or more consecutive days to the upside, and then a narrow range bar forms after

FIGURE 7.1 - PBS and NRB

Pristine Buy Setup    +    NRB/NB         Result
(PBS)

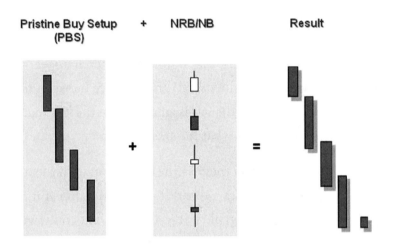

**Pristine Trading Combo 3**

For color charts go to www.traderslibrary.com/TLEcorner

this move to the upside, this is a strong indication that the stock is poised to move back to the downside.

One final fact to understand and definitely keep in mind about narrow range days is this; moves that occur from narrow range bars, tend to be far more explosive than moves from normal range bars. I want you to think of the narrow range bar like a soda bottle that

> The narrow range bar is just one of many combo tactics, and it can increase the reliability and profitability of the trade in three different ways.

you shake. When the top gets popped, an explosion happens. That bar is contained with so much pressure that it acts like a spring that when released will have a violent move one way or the other. Moves that occur from narrow range bars are far more potent than moves that occur from normal range bars.

Here is one more thing to consider about the narrow range bar. Remember where my stop is going to be? My entry is based off the high of the narrow range bar on the following day, and the stop will be the lower of the narrow range bar or my entry bar. This means the stock will be very small. This, of course, gives me a high reward to risk ratio on the trade. The small stop, the likely explosive move and the reliability of the shift in momentum in progress makes this a high odds play, and a reason to increase your share size above the normal amount.

> Power trading combos can increase the reliability and profitability of both income producing and wealth building strategies. There are many to learn, which are beyond the scope of this book.

Here is one more thing about the narrow range bar. If one narrow range bar is powerful, two are more powerful. Not only that, another clue is to look at who won the second narrow range day. Who won? The buyers or sellers? If that second narrow bar actually turns white, we know that we have more than a slowing of momentum. We have a shift in power to the bulls.

There are many other combos that I teach my traders that range from volume to trend lines to support concepts. They all hope to enhance the reliability of this already very reliable tactic.

There are a few other items I would like to mention before concluding this book. While this book has discussed swing trading, these strategies actually work on any timeframe. Every timeframe looks identical except for the ledger on the chart. Also, these strategies work on anything that can be bought and sold in the open market. High volatility stocks, low volatility stocks, corn futures, Forex, or the market itself, it does not matter. The reason: we trade people. Prices move based on supply and demand, which is controlled by the emotions of the people pushing the buttons. Greed, uncertainty, fear, and ambivalence. Over and over again.

> These strategies can be applied to anything that is bought and sold and on any timeframe.

I also want to remind you that every strategy discussed applies to shorting a stock just as well as going long. I have used the bullish bias example throughout this book because it is more easily understood by most people. Unfortunately, this only promotes the general tendency for people to have a bullish bias.

## Stay With Your Plan

Be sure to prepare properly for the market every day and follow-up on all of your trades. One of the issues you will encounter after taking a trade is whether or not you followed the proper procedures in selecting and executing a play. After all, I will not be there looking over your shoulder to correct you if you do something wrong. It is up to you to compare your selections to the criteria outlined in this course book. You also need to make sure you have a trading plan that outlines the strategies you are going to trade, in the timeframe you are going to trade them, and with proper money management guidelines. It is recommended that you start off paper trading to learn any strategy that is new to you. Once you are successful paper trading, you may begin trading small shares with a small risk amount until you've proven to be successful.

Finally, there is no greater educator than experience. You will go through your ups and downs as everyone does to some degree. You need to make sure you keep your capital in place until you are successful. Trading is based on odds and requires much discipline. Do not ever take the market for granted. Follow your rules and treat trading as the business that it is.

# Self-test questions

1. Once you decide on a universe of stocks to trade, what do you look for?

   a. Three black bars or three white bars
   b. Uptrends and downtrends
   c. Low P/E numbers
   d. Narrow range bars, two in a row are best

2. Which of the following are power trading combos discussed in the book?

   a. Guerilla tactics
   b. Gaps
   c. Narrow range days
   d. 52-week highs

3. What do you do once you've established a hot list for the day?

   a. Wait for micro reversals to occur, then buy
   b. Place buy orders on the strongest trending stocks
   c. Wait 30 minutes past opening, then buy the strongest stocks
   d. Do nothing, wait until tomorrow for confirmation

4. Why are narrow range bars exceptionally powerful?

   a. The narrow range shows a lack of trader interest, and the stock will not "blow up" on you
   b. The color of the body tips off the future direction of the stock
   c. A lower risk/reward with the small candlestick body
   d. They are infallible in predicting a reversal

5. Name a limitation when using the Prisitine method:

   a. Can only trade stocks and futures markets
   b. Limited to 2-5 day trades
   c. Can only trade momentum stocks in trends
   d. There are no limitations—fear and greed exist in all open market trading systems

**For answers, go to www.traderslibrary.com/TLEcorner**

# Chapter 8

# Chart Lessons

## The Pristine Method Adapts to the Market in More Ways Than One

One of the remarkable features of the Pristine Method® of Trading is that it works on any instrument that can be bought and sold. There is a reason for that. Take a look at all the debacles in history. Whether it is the famous Tulip crisis, the Great Depression, the Nifty-Fifty, the Internet Craze of the 90s, or any other time, they all have something in common. The same chart pattern. How can tulip bulbs trade the same as Internet stocks? What do they have in common? They have in common only one thing; the people that trade them. Their emotions are what form the chart patterns. For this reason the Pristine Method® works on everything, including the market itself.

## What is the Market?

It is interesting how we throw the term market around, yet it is rarely defined. Well, let's start from the top. The market generally means the whole stock market. There are three main exchanges that trade the vast majority of all stocks. They are the New York Stock Exchange (NYSE), the NASDAQ Stock Exchange, and the American Stock Exchange (AMEX). While the numbers change, the NASDAQ is the largest currently with about 3,300 stocks trading. The NYSE is next with about 2,700, and the AMEX last with about 800.

It is more common, however, to view the market through the eyes of an index. This is a list of the larger, key stocks that are thought to be representative of the market itself. Some indices you might have heard of are the S&P 500, the NASDAQ 100, and the Dow Industrials (Dow).

The S&P 500 is widely regarded as the best single gauge of the U.S. equities market. It is a representative sample of 500 leading companies in leading industries of the U.S. economy. The S&P 500 focuses on the large-cap segment of the market, with over 80% coverage of U.S. equities. It is an ideal proxy for the total market. To view the actual price and chart of the S&P 500, you put in the symbol for the cash index. For example, on many charting packages that symbol is $INX.X.

The NASDAQ 100 Index includes 100 of the largest domestic and international non-financial companies listed on The NASDAQ

Stock Market based on market capitalization. The NASDAQ 100 reflects companies across major industry groups including computer hardware and software, telecommunications, retail/wholesale trade, and biotechnology. To view the actual price and chart of the NASDAQ 100, you put in the symbol for the cash index. For example, on many charting packages that symbol is $NDX.X.

The Dow is an index of only 30 stocks that is thought to be a cross section of our entire market. It is often used as the representative of the U.S. Market globally. It is maintained and reviewed by editors of *The Wall Street Journal.* For the sake of continuity, composition changes are rare and generally occur only after corporate acquisitions or other dramatic shifts in a component's core business. To view the actual price and chart of the Dow, you put in the symbol for the cash index. For example, on many charting packages that symbol is $DJI.

Note that there can be overlap. Intel Corp. (INTC) for example, is in the NASDAQ 100, S&P 500, and the Dow.

There are also HOLDRS and ETFs, which are often confused. HOLDRS (spelled correctly even though it is pronounced as 'holders') is an acronym for HOLding Company Depositary ReceiptS and are a product of Merrill Lynch & Co., Inc. They are securities that represent an investor's ownership in the common stock or American Depositary Receipts of specified companies in a particular industry, sector, or group. In other words, they are traded like a single stock but represent ownership in several stocks in a sector in most cases. Some common HOLDRS that traders use are BBH for the Biotech sector and HHH for the Internet sector.

ETF is an acronym for Exchange Traded Fund. Each ETF is a basket of securities that is designed to generally track an index (stock or bond, stock industry sector, or international stock), yet trades like a single stock. There are more than 120 ETFs, and the most common ones traders use are the QQQ, SPY, and DIA. These are the ETFs for the NASDAQ 100, S&P 500, and Dow Industrials.

In addition to the above, there are also futures. A futures contract is an obligation to receive or deliver a commodity or financial instrument sometime in the future, but at a price that's agreed upon today. People commonly think of futures in corn and pork bellies. But futures have also been developed for financial markets. As you might guess, there are futures for the NASDAQ 100, S&P 500, and the Dow. To view these you must be permissioned to receive futures quotes (talk to your broker). Symbols often look like /NDH6, /SPH6, and /ZDH6, respectively (by the way, the S&P Futures is the one that carries the nick-name "spoos"). Note, the last two characters ("H6") represent the month and year of the future and change every quarter.

The most popular financial futures contracts were set up as new trading instruments by reducing their size. This setup a series of products known as the E-minis. They are available for the NASDAQ 100, S&P 500, and the Dow. Their symbols are /NQH6,

/ESH6, and /YMH6 respectively. They are popular due to the reduced size and requirements.

So, how many ways could you view the S&P 500? Well, there is the cash index ($INX.X), the Electronically Traded Fund (SPY), the future (/SPH6), the E-mini future (/ESH6). Is there any difference in the chart patterns? Well, they are all tied to the same underlying instrument, the price action of the S&P 500, so at the end of the day the chart patterns will all be similar. However, depending on what is happening in the market, the intraday price action may vary slightly as one of these may begin to move ahead of the others.

So when you hear someone just say the market, they are likely referring to whatever they last discussed, or they may be just using the term in a generic way to describe the action of all stocks. There will often be very different patterns when you compare the NASDAQ to the S&P 500, or any other individual sector. Sometimes they will look similar. However, whatever instrument you use to view the S&P 500, be it the cash index, the ETF, the futures (spoos), or the E-minis, they will look similar at the end of the day. That is because they are all viewing the same instrument, that same basket of 500 stocks.

## An Example of the Pristine Method in Action

Let's start off with an example of the Pristine Method® of Trading as applied to the market itself, using the concepts taught in this book. Look at Figure 8.1. This is a chart of the SPY, which is the ETF for the S&P 500. So we are viewing the largest index of the total market. I did not look long for this chart; it is the current picture of the market at the time of the writing of this book.

Notice the overall pattern of this chart. Remember for the uptrend, we want higher highs on the rallies and higher lows on the

---

**FIGURE 8.1 - SPY Daily Chart**

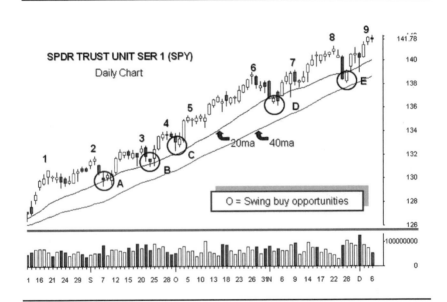

For color charts go to www.traderslibrary.com/TLEcorner

---

pullbacks. Most of the higher highs are numbered 1-9 and most of the higher lows are letters A-E. The rising 20-period moving average (r20ma) is there, as is the rising 40-period moving average (r40ma.) There is a nice even space between the moving averages. We have our uptrend.

Once we have our uptrend established, I want you to notice how the stock responds to the r20ma. This is a very common occurrence in the sign of a bullish uptrend. You can literally buy the stock every time it touches the r20ma and make money. Naturally, that would not lead to good money management practices because there is not a clear entry or exit strategy. This is why we use the Pristine Buy Setup in the area of the rising 20-period moving average Every higher low that forms in the area of the r20ma is buyable. The five circles are all pullbacks to the rising 20-period moving average. All but one if them is a Pristine Buy Setup. Take a look at the chart for a minute and see if you can tell which one it is.

The only circle that did not form a true PBS is circle B. This is because the pullback only contains two black bars and two lower highs. Again I want to emphasize that this chart is the S&P 500 at the time of this writing. The Pristine Method® of Trading works on anything that can be bought and sold including the indices and the market itself.

Let's take a look at an example of another huge concept from this course book, the basic unit of any stock. Remember that all stocks and every market always go through the four stages. They have to, there is no other choice. What you'll find as you begin trading is that some of the patterns are crystal clear as they develop, and some are not as clear until after the pattern is complete. Naturally, the reason we scan is to seek out the patterns that are crystal clear as they are forming, but not the ones that are ambiguous until after the fact. Figure 8.2 is a chart of KLA-Tencor Corp., a big named tech stock that engages in the design, manufacture, and marketing of process monitoring systems for the semiconductor industry.

Coming into late May KLAC is in a free falling stage four downtrend. Notice that at the end of a long decline, the stock gaps down

---

**FIGURE 8.2 - KLA Daily Chart**

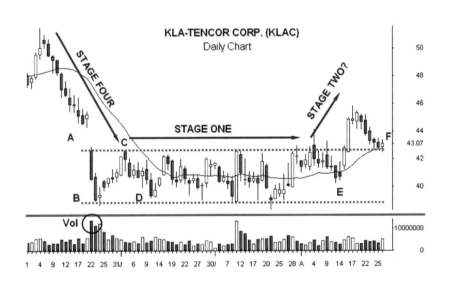

For color charts go to www.traderslibrary.com/TLEcorner

at A and trades with the two largest black bars on the chart on huge volume (B). While it is beyond the scope of this book, this is what we call a novice move and will often set the bottom and end downtrends. That is exactly what happens in this case. The stock then rallies to C before trading back down to D to retest the low that was just set. From there, points C and D form the top and bottom of the stage one base that develops. Again, while it is beyond the scope of this book to discuss, there is a whole other area to learn known as transitional analysis that helps you determine how and where Points C and D will be set in and why point C is not a shortable event.

Notice how long this sideways action continues with very similar highs and lows. Finally at point E we get a hint of what is coming. A low is formed at a point that is significantly higher than the bottom of the established base. The rally leaving point E has wide white bars that break through the top of the stage one consolidation. In transitional analysis you will discover that that first pullback at point F can be an excellent entry even though we have not yet established a stage 2 uptrend. The bottoming process is now complete and stage two will continue to take the stock higher.

Let's take a look at some more examples of how stocks change stages. It is a very important concept because one of the greatest mistakes traders make is trying to catch a free falling stock rather than waiting for the transition to a new stage. Figure 8.3 is a chart of Myogen Inc., a therapeutic company.

FIGURE 8.3 - Myogen Daily Chart.

For color charts go to www.traderslibrary.com/TLEcorner

Again, we have a stock that has been in a downtrend as it comes into the chart on the left side. The stock continues its fall until we get the first clue that a change of stage is coming. The wide white bar that develops at point A on huge volume is known as a professional wide range bar, and it is very likely going to end the current downtrend. Notice also that in the rally to B it traded above a lower low represented by the line. The next pullback to the area at C forms a higher low, and we now have a higher high and higher low in place. The stock then gaps out of this area on professional volume to D which now puts us in a stage two, where the next pullback will be buyable. This chart is very different than Figure 8.2 because the stage one shown here is a very short period of time. Stage one lasts long enough only to trade one higher high and one higher low. In other words point A becomes a type of V bottom as sometimes is the case with stage one.

Notice that the first pullback after the attempt to move into stage two at point E is a very sloppy area with many sideways bars. This is often the case until the uptrend is clearly defined as you see on the pullbacks and Pristine Buy Setups at points F and G.

I hope these charts are driving home some other concepts of this book by example. One of the secrets to your success will be to continue to look at charts such as these and analyze them, as I am doing for you. These are not unique charts that I had to search for. They are common to find, but remember not every chart will look as clean and neat. Your job as a swing trader is to find the charts where the stock or index is clearly tipping its hand with clear entries.

If you remember, I discussed the fact that we use combinations to help enhance our setups. I gave you an example of one known as a narrow range bar (NRB). Figure 8.4 is a chart that shows the narrow range bar being used in the Pristine Buy Setup, which is the first set up formed in a newly developed stage two uptrend after transitioning from stage four to stage one to stage two. It is a chart of the restaurant known as Ruby Tuesday's.

The stock is then in a serious downtrend where every rally and every consolidation has been shortable. The downtrend continues

FIGURE 8.4 - Ruby Tuesday's daily Chart

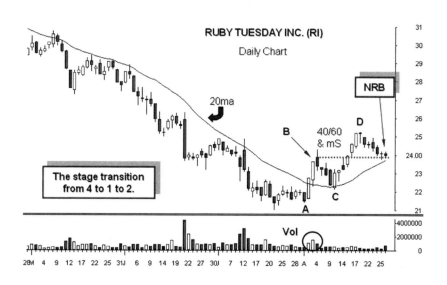

and at point A, you should be ready to short the break down once it trades under that small base that is formed. However; instead of trading down, the stock rallies with a wide white bar and trades above the base and the last lower high of the downtrend. I am not saying that the stock was necessarily buyable on that rally as a swing trade, but I am saying that bar has ended the downtrend and the ensuing rally was significant enough, with large volume, that an aggressive trader would play the transition by going long on the Pristine Buy Set up at C.

FIGURE 8.5 - United States Oil Fund Daily Chart.

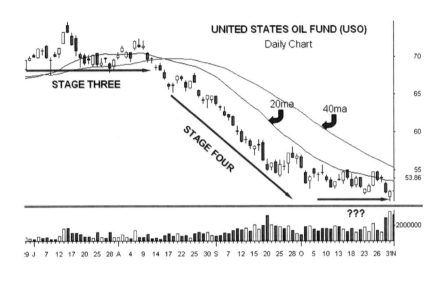

The next rally takes us to a new high at D, and we now have our official stage 2 uptrend beginning. The moving averages have not fallen in place yet, but we now have two higher highs and the next pullback possibly setting up the second higher low. That next pullback forms a very nice Pristine Buy Set up with a narrow range bar. In addition there are other combinations here that make this a very nice set up.

In Figure 8.5 there are two final points I want to make. One of them is to remind you that these swing trading tactics work on anything that can be bought and sold. I am often asked if these concepts work on futures, Forex, and a whole list of all other securities. They do. This chart is a chart of the price of oil as represented by the ETF of the United States Oil Fund, symbol USO. While oil and oil stocks will certainly trade independent of the stock market, they will still go through their own stages like any other security. Note the ambivalence present in stage three and the fear in stage four that produces the dramatic decline. A bottom is formed for now, and our job as swing traders will be to determine if that area with the question marks will become a pause in stage four or a stage one, which will produce higher prices.

I want to call your attention to the fact that while this chart goes through the stages it is not as neat and orderly during stage four. It is not easy to find 3 bar rallies, and you see areas where there are gaps between the bars and some are overlapping. This is simply a function of the fact that oil trades twenty-four hours a day; so, the U.S. Market picks up the opening price while it is being actively traded.

The second item I want to discuss is to remind you that this chart features a stage four downtrend. It is your job to short rallies and consolidation breakdowns in downtrends just as easily as you buy pullbacks and consolidation breakouts in uptrends. Other charts in this chapter happen to feature the transition from a downtrend to a sideways trend to an uptrend, but you should be just as eager to find the transition from an uptrend to a sideways trend to a downtrend.

## In Conclusion...Practice Makes Perfect

A key for you will be to take this information and practice until these patterns become obvious to you. Charts speak their own language. At times they whisper, and at times they are screaming at us. Like any language, it must be learned, and the better you are at the language, the better you can communicate. In the stock market, that is priceless.

# Self-test questions

1. What is the S&P 500?

   a. A stock exchange
   b. An index
   c. SPOOS
   d. An ETF

2. What are you trading if you've own YMH4s?

   a. E-minis
   b  HOLDRS
   c. NASDAQ
   d. Futures

3. In the Pristine system, which is the cleanest chart set-up?

   a. A gap down following three black bars in a down-trending stock
   b. Three black bars in a Stage 2 stock; the moving averages look like railroad tracks
   c. Three white bars followed by a narrow range bar in a side-ways-trading stock
   d. A gap below the 20-day moving average in a stock in a clearly defined uptrend

4. Which set-up would be the hardest to trade?

    a. Three white bars in a sideways-trading stock, with the 20-day moving average crossing over the 40-day moving average
    b. Three white bars in a downtrending stock followed by a gap down
    c. Three black bars in an uptrend followed by the stock opening and trading higher than the previous day's high
    d. A free falling stock

5. An aggressive trader can enter a Pristine short set-up when:

    a. A stock in an uptrend passes the targeted previous high, then trades below yesterday's low
    b. Three lower lows and three lower highs form, thus establishing a downtrend
    c. Three black bars following two lower lows in a Stage 3 stock
    d. Two lower lows and two lower highs form

**For answers, go to www.traderslibrary.com/TLEcorner**

# Trading Resource Guide

# RECOMMENDED READING

## STRATEGIES FOR PROFITING ON EVERY TRADE
### by Oliver Velez

An accessible, reliable course for the trader looking for profits in the competitive, dynamic world of trading.

Each section of the book offers clear examples, concise and useful definitions of important terms, over 90 charts used to illustrate the challenges and opportunities of the market; and how you can take advantage of patterns. Written in the parlance of the day trader's world, you'll enjoy the experience of being taught trading skills by the best of the best.

This focused and effective trading resource features seven key lessons to further a trader's education including market basics, managing trades, psychology in trading and planning, technicals, utilizing charts, income versus wealth building producing trades, and classic patterns. It truly is as Paul Lange says, "Many of these lessons have been taught to students worldwide over a span of 4 years. These lessons contain powerful information that goes far beyond the basics you may find in many introductory trading books."

Item #BCOVx5031652- $49.95

# 5 TRADING TACTICS THAT BEAT THE MARKET
## *by Oliver Velez*

Finding profits in today's markets can be overwhelming. Now, one of the most sought after educators in the industry, Oliver Velez, cuts through the noise and hands you the five tactics that will get you to winning trades. From clearly seeing the trends in the chaos of market, to zeroing in on plays that are about to breakout and the key to significantly minimizing losses—this course hands you 5 of the most effective weapons to beat the markets.

Item #BCOVx5197571 - $99.00

# TOOLS AND TACTICS FOR THE MASTER DAYTRADER: BATTLE-TESTED TECHNIQUES FOR DAY, SWING, AND POSITION TRADERS 1ST EDITION
## *by Oliver Velez and Greg Capra*

A no-nonsense, straight-shooting guide from the founder of Pristine. com, designed for active, self-directed traders. Provides potent trading strategies, technical skills, intuitive insights on discipline, psychology and winning methods for capturing more winning trades, more often.

Item #BCOVx11221 - $55.00

# MARKET WIZARDS
## *by Jack D. Schwager*

What fellow traders are saying about Market Wizards:

"Market Wizards is one of the most fascinating books ever written about Wall Street. A few of the "Wizards" are my friends—and Jack Schwager has nailed their modus operandi on the head."

> - Martin W. Zweig, Ph.D., Editor
> The Zweig Forecast

"It's difficult enough to develop a method that works. It then takes experience to believe what your method is telling you. But the toughest task of all is turning analysis into money. If you don't believe it, try it. These guys have it all: a method, the conviction and the discipline to act decisively time after time, regardless of distractions and pressures. They are heroes of Wall Street, and Jack Schwager's book brings their characters vividly to life."

> - Robert R. Prechter, Jr., Editor of The
> Elliott Wave Theorist

> Item #BCOVx4050480 - $17.95

## JAPANESE CANDLESTICK CHARTING TECHNIQUES, 2ND EDITION
### *by Steve Nison*

This easy-to-read guide provides a clear understanding of Japanese Candlestick Charting, an increasingly popular and dynamic approach to market analysis. Steve Nison, known around the world as the "Father of Candlesticks, uses hundreds of examples that show how candlestick techniques can be used in all of today's markets. Traders will learn how candlestick charting can be used to improve returns and help decrease market risk.

Item #BCOVx 17304 - $100.00

## To get the current lowest price on any item listed
# Go to www.traderslibrary.com

# Free 2 Week Trial Offer for U.S. Residents From Investor's Business Daily:

**I**NVESTOR'S BUSINESS DAILY will provide you with the facts, figures, and objective news analysis you need to succeed.

*Investor's Business Daily* is formatted for a quick and concise read to help you make informed and profitable decisions.

To take advantage of this free 2 week trial offer,
e-mail us at customerservice@fpbooks.com
or visit our website at www.fpbooks.com where
you find other free offers as well.

You can also reach us by calling 1-800-272-2855
or fax us at 410-964-0027.

This book, along with other books, is available at discounts that make it realistic to provide it as a gift to your customers, clients, and staff. For more information on these long lasting, cost effective premiums, please call us at (800) 272-2855 or you may email us at sales@traderslibrary.com.